AF209842

FSC
www.fsc.org

MIX

Papier aus ver-
antwortungsvollen
Quellen

Paper from
responsible sources

FSC® C105338

NO

ANDREAS MÜLLER
JUSTIN ALLEN

Imprint

Impressum

Bibliografische Information der Deutschen Nationalbibliothek: Die Deutsche Nationalbibliothek verzeichnet diese Publikation in der Deutschen Nationalbibliografie; detaillierte bibliografische Daten sind im internet über www.dnd.de abrufbar.

Bibliographic information from the German National Library: The German National Library lists this publication in the German National Bibliography; detailed bibliographic data are available on the Internet at www.dnb.de.

COPYRIGHT: 2024 Justin Allen and Andreas Müller

Cover: © Justin Allen

Layout and editing: © Justin Allen

Illustrations: © Justin Allen

Verlag: BoD · Books on Demand GmbH, In de Tarpen 42, 22848 Norderstedt

Druck: Libri Plureos GmbH, Friedensallee 273, 22763 Hamburg

ISBN: 978-3-7693-1287-4

Acknowledgements from Andreas Müller:

Thanks to Vivien Thomas, Soham, Tony and Claire Parsons

Acknowledgements from Justin Allen:

Thanks to my family, close and far friends and Andreas

CONTENTS

September 21, 2024   JUSTIN ALLEN

PREFACE

This is the final installment in our trilogy of talks about nothing. Or, more accurately, talks that circle around the "no-point," the elusive space where words and concepts dissolve. If the first book, "No-Point Perspective," (2020) laid out the vast landscape of this terrain, and the second, "No-Point," (2022) narrowed the focus (not really), then this one, "No," (2024) is a pinprick of light, a whisper in the nothingness.

We've gone from fourteen talks to seven, and now to a mere three and a half (or maybe four, depending on how you count). We've moved from the disembodied realm of Skype and telephone to the tangible presence of Andreas' village, a place where the rolling hills and quaint houses seem to reflect the ordinary we're pointing towards.

Face to face, I found myself running out of things to say. The words that flowed so freely in previous conversations seemed to stumble and fall silent in the face of the actual. And yet, in that silence, something shifted. The "no-point" wasn't just an idea anymore, it was the air we breathed, the space between us.

Even the title of this book became a point of contention, a playful dance around the edges of meaning. "No" seemed too absolute, too one-sided. "No-(Yes)" hinted at the paradox, the refusal to settle on any fixed position. But in the end, we circled back to the simplicity of "No." Not as a negation, but as a disregard to meaning or point, other than to follow the natural course of subtracting from our original title – No-Point Perspective.

This is not a book to be understood, it can't be. It's a final bow, a gentle nudge towards the precipice of the "no-point." And then, a step off.

INTRODUCTION

After having done two books already with Justin, I am very happy that this third and last book of our trilogy happened. I very much enjoyed Justin's visit to my place and the open and warm atmosphere in which our conversations happened. Justin is a lovely person who's certainly very interesting to talk to. His questions were sincere and showed his deep interest and resonance with this apparent issue that we call "non-duality." Such a joy.

BREAD CRUMB

Justin Allen:	Okay, this is our first talk in person, and it's the 8th of February. So this is our third time (22nd time) putting together some kind of a talk, but we're doing it live together face to face. And I'm in your village. And just to describe it, it's a small village in the south of Germany. And it's what I would say is an average kind of apartment by German standards. And I came from Berlin, and we will do this for two days. So, this is our first conversation.
Andreas Müller:	Yeah. Lovely. Welcome.
Justin Allen:	Thank you. I guess what occurred to me was that I hadn't come prepared for this talk. And like the other ones that we had, I also didn't really prepare stuff, but I had a motivation and I had things that I had wanted to ask for a long time. So I think this discussion might be a little bit unusual only because I don't have contrived or premeditated provocations.
Andreas Müller:	(laughs) I haven't noticed that the former ones were provocations, actually, but yes.
Justin Allen:	The other thing is that last night we met and we had dinner. And we talked about things, in a sense, unrelated to this topic, where I got a little bit more of a sense of your life. But from that point until now, and then on the train ride here, I had a couple of

thoughts and I wrote them down on my phone. I don't want to bring them up yet. It doesn't feel like the right time. But I have some. Those are the two contrived (laughs) premeditated things that I've thought of.

I thought it would be interesting to just start by saying that we're here. We're looking at each other, and there's no difference between us, or there's no difference in the sense that you are there and I'm here.

Andreas Müller: Yes.

Justin Allen: So, from your point of view, there's no differentiation because there's no two different entities that are here talking to each other.

Andreas Müller: Absolutely. Yeah. One could say so. It's not really my perspective on something or my viewpoint, but this experience isn't happening here.

Justin Allen: From your point of view, it's not happening to me either, even if I claim that it is.

Andreas Müller: Exactly. And what's recognized is this claim. So this claim is what seems to be happening, but there isn't any reality of that recognized.

Justin Allen: So if there's a distinction between us, it would only be, in this case, when I claim that I'm somebody here. And that's an illusion from your point of view, that somebody is here claiming that they're there.

Andreas Müller: Exactly. And that this claim is real, and creates a real separation or a real difference. Even your claim to be someone doesn't create a difference for me.

Justin Allen: But the claim, me claiming that I'm here, is as real as the window and the...

Andreas Müller:	Absolutely, yes

Justin Allen: But that I'm actually here is the thing that isn't happening. But the window is still happening.

Andreas Müller: Apparently. And you, and, all this body, Justin, claiming to be a "me," that's also like the window or like everything else. And it's not right or wrong. When I say it's an illusion that there is someone, I don't mean that I think it's wrong that you claim to be someone. There just isn't anyone, even in that claim.

Justin Allen: So, however, we go from there. That's the foundation, that there's apparently people claiming to be there, and you're reacting to those claims. In your discussions, I mean.

Andreas Müller: Absolutely, yeah, one could say so.

Justin Allen: And I thought of this just five minutes before we started, but then I wanted to start with that because in order for us to have this conversation, there has to be some sense of somebody here claiming to be a person. Or if there wasn't, let's say that it's another "no me" over here on the other side of the table from you. Where would this go?

Andreas Müller: I have no idea. There is no uh, (laughs) predictable outcome. I don't know how we would end up after those one and a half hours. But, yeah, there wouldn't be seeking.

Justin Allen: In general, what I'm saying is that it seems unlikely and not often happening that, for example, you and Tony Parsons are sitting across from each other and recording a conversation about nobody being here.

Andreas Müller: I would say this wouldn't happen.

Justin Allen:	And it hasn't happened.
Andreas Müller:	It hasn't happened, and I think it can't happen, actually. It would be so off to have this idea to sit down together and have a conversation about non-duality, and even record it, thinking that others...No, I don't see this at all.
Justin Allen:	So that's what I want to point out is that our synopsis of the first book was about, you not being there, me being there, and us having a conversation. And this third conversation that we're having now still has that same kind of pretext or foundation.
Andreas Müller:	Well, If you tell me now that you still claim to be someone, then it's going to be...
Justin Allen:	But I think I also don't know how this conversation will go, but, in a way, by default, I have to be the person that's here. You're not here, and I have to be the person who's here to engage in a conversation with you about non-duality.
Andreas Müller:	Yeah, one could say so.
Justin Allen:	But aside from confessing if I'm here… (laughs)
Andreas Müller:	I mean, of course, there could still be a conversation about non-duality when there is "no one." But, of course, it wouldn't be meaningful or important. It would just be playing around with ideas and concepts and viewpoints, which are all illusory. It's not that I never talk about non-dual concepts in my life outside of the meetings, but they don't have any meaning. Talking could also be any other topic.
Justin Allen:	But they don't have any meaning anyway, either.
Andreas Müller:	That's true, of course.

Justin Allen:	By you using the word meaning, to me, that just implies that if it's two "no me's" or "non me's" talking to each other about this topic, you said there's no meaning. But if there's "no me" talking to an audience of 10 people who are claiming to be there, there's also no meaning.
Andreas Müller:	There's also no meaning.
Justin Allen:	But by you saying that there's no meaning with two "no me's" talking, that implies that maybe there is meaning. And what I think you're implying is that there's meaning on the other side.
Andreas Müller:	Or the hope for meaning, or the illusion of meaning. Exactly. And, of course, the person thinks that to me, it's somehow meaningful as well. As we sit together here, have those microphones, or in a meeting as if it is meaningful, because that's why we meet consciously and talk about it.
Justin Allen:	That was an attempt in a way for me to try to make a definition of our roles or who we are here talking to each other. And even though it's not a claim, I'm going to use the word claim because there's a lack of a word to express this. But you are claiming to not be there.
Andreas Müller:	No.
Justin Allen:	But you know what I mean. (laughs)
Andreas Müller:	(laughs) I know what you mean, but that's just not the case.
Justin Allen:	But it's a case that you would say, "I'm just not here. There's nobody here."
Andreas Müller:	There's just no illusion to be someone.

Justin Allen:	That's why I'm using the word "claim." It's not that you have to define yourself or try to explain, but you also equally have to try to explain yourself and describe it to communicate with other people.
Andreas Müller:	But only in this context. The person would regard it as a claim that I present my experience here, which then would be in the absence or not being someone. And I'm sitting here saying, "This is my truth." It's not like that, of course,
Justin Allen:	It's not like that, but you can't avoid it in having conversations with people.
Andreas Müller:	Absolutely.
Justin Allen:	And so acknowledging that, then going forward, you're on the side of the table saying that there's nobody there, of being in this category in a way of accepting or acknowledging that there's just...
Andreas Müller:	In the meeting, so to speak, that's the accepted story.
Justin Allen:	Yes. And on the other side of the table are people that think they're there, that there's an identity and something there.
Andreas Müller:	Mostly, yeah.
Justin Allen:	Let's just say 90 percent, to avoid the exception to the rule.
Andreas Müller:	Yeah, most people are seeking...
Justin Allen:	To keep it in a more dual setting, is that they claim to be there. You don't claim to be there.
Andreas Müller:	Yeah, this claim isn't happening here.

Justin Allen:	So even that, you could say there's no claim, on your side of the table. And then there's a claim on the other side of the table.
Andreas Müller:	Exactly, and the claim is, I am someone, we are someone. We are seeking, we need an answer.
Justin Allen:	And then to try to define myself in this scenario, then I would say that... (laughs)
Andreas Müller:	(laughs) Yeah, who are you?
Justin Allen:	Yeah. I would want to probably... (know/hear the) answer you give, but I still think it's different. And my answer would be...that I wouldn't want to be held responsible for claiming that I'm here or not here. Meaning that I find it difficult... I feel like you can confidently go to a meeting and sit in front of 10 people and tell them that there's nothing there. There's nobody.
Andreas Müller:	No. And that's the thing, it's exactly not like that. It's not the same, because it's not that I don't want to define myself either this way or the other way. There is just no one here. But I don't go to a meeting and I'm confident with that claim. I don't go to a meeting and think beforehand, "Oh great, I told them that I'm no one and stuff." It doesn't happen actually, so it's rather a response than confident knowledge. Because I also can't say that there is no one.
Justin Allen:	Okay.
Andreas Müller:	And I can't say that exactly because there is no one. It's so direct.
Justin Allen:	But for example, if I'm hanging out with my brother, who I've known my whole life, and my brother is talking to me as if he believes that he's there and he's dealing with some problem or even something

that's not a problem. Whatever he's relating to, it's clear that he's relating to it from a point of view that he thinks that he's there and he's talking to me and maybe asking me for my point of view or advice. I don't know if I would say to him, "You are not there." I just wouldn't have this kind of confidence that it's one way or the other. Do you know what I mean?

Andreas Müller: Mm hmm.

Justin Allen: It can seem obvious in a way that, yeah, nobody's there. I would feel confident saying that that tree's there, even though I can entertain... also the possibility if it's really there. But saying that there's somebody inside...it's a little bit like God. Like for me, even from very early on, this idea of God never made sense to me. If a God-like figure is there or not, it's just Irrelevant.

Andreas Müller: Irrelevant, Yeah, you don't know, but it's irrelevant.

Justin Allen: It's like, air. In a way, air doesn't exist to me. You can't touch it, you can't see it, and it just doesn't play any role in my life at all,

Andreas Müller: Okay. (laughs) Though you are living from it. But I know what you mean.

Justin Allen: Or blackness.

Andreas Müller: Yeah, I know what you mean. You can't...

Justin Allen: And the tree, because I can touch it and I've done things with it and I can see it, then it's more there to me than God would be, let's say.

Andreas Müller: Yeah, I understand. Yeah.

Justin Allen: I can understand this idea of a "me" in the sense that I could say I felt very powerfully that I'm there at times. If something happens to me and I am going to the hospital and I have my leg cut, I think this is happening to me that my legs cut and the pain is happening to me. And then I could also be somebody that simultaneously is experiencing that and thinking that they're experiencing that, but also not sure if I'm there really experiencing this or if it's happening. I just wonder... you say it's so obvious that nobody's there, that there's not an experience.

Andreas Müller: Yeah. It's so natural. Let's put it like this.

Justin Allen: And for me, it's natural that God's not there and never existed, will never exist. All this is just natural. I don't spend any time questioning that.

Andreas Müller: It doesn't play a role in your life basically, yeah.

Justin Allen: And then in your meetings, some people ask you questions. And it seems obvious in the way that you're talking about a "me," like the way that you define what it's like to be a "me," that there are people who identify and feel like there's a "me." And then it sometimes seems like there are people that... I don't know if accept is the right word because accept still implies that there's a "me" they're accepting. But they seem to get it.

Andreas Müller: Yeah, absolutely.

Justin Allen: Where, I feel like they wouldn't confidently say, " I know I'm here." They might still feel themselves there in some way.

Andreas Müller: Yeah, but the conviction about "I am here" is kind of already broken.

Justin Allen: Exactly. And the way that we just talked about it, then I could imagine somebody hearing this and start to think, ah, there are stages. So you're there as a "me." And then at some point, you're like, "Oh, maybe this "me" thing that I've been feeling isn't..."

Andreas Müller: (laughs) Yeah.

Justin Allen: That type of person is in stage two. And then stage three is maybe where they start to become disillusioned with that sense of "me," where they react angrily. And before, they would always feel internally, like, "Oh, I'm angry, and this shouldn't happen to me." And then they detach themselves a little bit from that where they still have anger, but then it just doesn't feel the same way as before, where they're holding on to it in some way.

Andreas Müller: Or where it had a deep impact on what they think their life is or something.

Justin Allen: But then they start to say, okay, well, I'm still eating food. I'm not stopping eating food, and I'm still getting angry sometimes, and I still want to move to another location sometimes. But that sense of there's a "me" or that there's somebody there that wants to do all this stuff isn't happening the same way as it used to be happening. Because of that, then they can't claim that they're there anymore.

Andreas Müller: Yeah.

Justin Allen: And that setting, then that would be stage three or four. I don't know what number I'm on. (laughs)

Andreas Müller: Yeah.

Justin Allen: And then if there's a final stage after that, it means that that "me," if it was just there as a little thing, isn't there anymore. It's completely gone. And then they're "you."

Andreas Müller:	(laughs) On the final stage. Oh yeah, I can easily imagine how many of those stories about stages and stuff came from that. It just isn't like that.
Justin Allen:	But also, the person would never know.
Andreas Müller:	That's the other thing, yeah. Sometimes I tell my story, I guess you know it, with the last two years of fading out or something. I tell this story like that, looking back. But it was never my experience when I was still someone, or in those two years of fading out. And it's so easy for the person to talk. It's to look for signs and to talk itself into a stage and think that I'm closer or less close. And all of that doesn't exist.
Justin Allen:	But that's what I mean too, is somebody claiming for sure that they're there…maybe if you take Santa Claus, you wrote a book about Santa Claus, right?
Andreas Müller:	Yeah, the thing is that there's just no advantage in that. So, that's why with this stage thing… but of course, there are, apparently, differences and changes in people's lives. As you said, when they met this message, they felt like a full-on "me," so to speak, and then after a while, they can't keep up that claim as easily anymore as before.
Justin Allen:	And then at some point, maybe they can't keep that claim up at all. And then, they'd be like "you."
Andreas Müller:	This would be liberation then.
Justin Allen:	Yeah.
Andreas Müller:	There wouldn't be anyone there anymore.
Justin Allen:	But as you say, and as we already said in this meeting today, there's nobody there ever. So even when there's this, what you call this apparent energy claiming from contraction to be there, it's not

there. The claim is apparently happening. Just like we said, the tree is apparently happening, but that there's some substance behind it is never happening.

Andreas Müller: That's why this whole idea of stage doesn't make sense. The personal world is so different, apparently, from the natural reality. So, when the person hears stages and this process, it already has this idea that there is an actual goal and that I'm on a path towards that. And that's just not happening. Also in those apparent stages, or those apparent states, a full-on "me" and less "me" or less beliefs, it's still not a stage on a path towards fulfillment or wholeness, or the actual goal, which would be not being anyone. All of that just is what seems to be happening. And all of that just is the impersonal natural reality.

Justin Allen: I think before it was more confusing and maybe now it's more interesting, as a concept, is thinking about how when liberation apparently happens, it's not liberation because you were liberated the whole time. It's kind of like, you're just saying that there's no life ever.

Andreas Müller: Yes.

Justin Allen: There's no life ever.

Andreas Müller: There's no me, ever. Yeah.

Justin Allen: So there's also no death ever.

Andreas Müller: Yes, exactly.

Justin Allen: That also means there's no liberation ever.

Andreas Müller: Absolutely.

Justin Allen:

That's why I'm using the word "claim" just as a way to differentiate things. But from your point of view, in reality, there's no differentiation.

Andreas Müller:

Exactly. And there is no liberation. And there is no claim here that I'm "no one" in opposition to your claim saying you are someone. Those aren't two claims that are opposed to each other.

Justin Allen:

If there were stages. If you just entertained the idea and said, okay, there… seem to be five stages that the person goes through. When the person reaches the final stage, they then realize there are no stages.

Andreas Müller:

Exactly.

Justin Allen:

And then if the person is in a stage, it means that something is there. It's claiming to be there.

Andreas Müller:

Exactly. In all those illusory stages, there would always be someone there claiming to be in one way or the other.

Justin Allen:

But in every stage, equally, no matter what, the person just isn't there in the first place.

Andreas Müller:

There isn't a real person there, because this illusion doesn't happen to someone. Exactly.

Justin Allen:

The stages, even from your perspective, are meaningless. But even from the person that thinks that they're in stages and going through stages, it's also in the reality that, from your point of view, it's equally as meaningless, even for that person. Because that person isn't there.

Andreas Müller:

Absolutely. It's a dreamt meaning that the illusion adds to that imagined state. It is meaningless, really. It's all meaningless. And those stages don't mean anything and they aren't bringing someone closer to wholeness or it's just not happening.

That's the funny thing, I think, because the seeker always thinks, "Yeah, my experience has some kind of reality." Yeah, there are people who, 100%, believe in being someone, and then there are some who don't do that much anymore. The seeker would instantly say, "Yeah, but that's better if you don't believe in it 100%. Isn't that closer to what you talk about? Isn't that closer to not being someone? Isn't it kind of meaningful in that sense?" And no, it isn't. It just isn't. It never is meaningful. And there never is someone on a path, no matter how much this is believed or...

Justin Allen: I think that you brought this up in our first 14 talks, but it could have been the second seven talks. Either way, it's stuck with me. When I have friends that are interested in this topic and they listen to you, or maybe they listen to somebody else. On their own, nothing to do with me. And when they meet me, sometimes they might want to talk about something. And then sometimes it happens that I come to this (message). I relate to them this conversation that you and I have. To put it simply, I think your line is something like, "When the "me" died, then I could be me."

Andreas Müller: Mm-Hmm. Yes. (laughs)

Justin Allen: And I think it's a nice sentence because it's paradoxical. But the way that I interpreted it was to use it as a hypothetical example: somebody's born, and then they go through "the normal life." And then, at the age of 20, they need to choose what to do. And this person wants to be a painter, let's say. But from 10 years to 20 years old, parents and the school that they went to and everybody said being a painter won't make money, and it's very unlikely to succeed. So, this person was never encouraged to become a painter. Instead, the parents and other factors put a lot of pressure on this person to become a doctor. And so when the person at 20 decides what to do, they end up choosing to become a doctor. And then they go and become a doctor, and they realize in the 20 years that it takes for them to actually make it to becoming a doctor that they've suffered. And they always had this underlying feeling when they had to make a decision, they were contemplating, "Should I be a painter or should I be a doctor?" And they couldn't tell which one (They are/were) I am. "Am I really a painter, or am I a doctor?" If I was truly a painter, then even this idea of becoming a doctor wouldn't happen. But because there was some doubt about being a painter and their part of me was saying, "No, become a doctor. It's a better life, and you help people." And so they became a doctor, and then 40 years old now, the person (the "me") dies and starts painting.

Andreas Müller: Yeah. (laughs) It's really a bit like that. Maybe not necessarily with this example, because this could also happen to a "me," the idea of something that I want, to others, and now... nowadays, I think the bookstores are full of people who found their true...

Justin Allen: Exactly, they've become a baker.

Andreas Müller: Yeah, exactly. So it's not really like that. But of course, as long as there is someone, life is trying to build around this need to fulfill oneself. This might be a bit similar to the picture that you made with the painter and the doctor because the "me" would just think I have to be a doctor because this fulfills me. And there just can't be what naturally happens. I mean, there wouldn't be this opposite thing of, "I actually want to be a painter." That would be the difference in liberation because this illusion of a personal life collapses.

Justin Allen:	Well, I meant it more like when the "me" dies in that scenario, then they start painting.
Andreas Müller:	Exactly, yeah. Then, suddenly, life isn't needed to fulfill the "me" again. And that's why life can also change when the "me" collapses. It doesn't have to. I know a lot of people where the "me" collapsed and basically, they stayed in the same situation they were in before. However, also there are slight changes or things that don't happen anymore where they thought they needed this. But, life can also dramatically change, or... well, it wouldn't be dramatic for the "no one," so to speak, but...
Justin Allen:	That's how I interpreted it. For you, you were on some kind of a path. The way that I think of it is that everybody has a certain character and certain personality traits.
Andreas Müller:	I think as long as there was someone, there was just Andreas, the seeker. Andreas was the seeker. The "me" and the seeker. And now, when there is "no one," there's just a character that plays out freely without any goal or without needing to have a life that fulfills its "me." And before that, it was always me having a character, trying to use the character, trying to control this body to create the life that I thought I needed.
Justin Allen:	Yeah, a person is going to have certain DNA characteristics.
Andreas Müller:	(laughs) But during all that time I liked spaghetti.
Justin Allen:	Yeah.
Andreas Müller:	That didn't change.
Justin Allen:	But it could have.
Andreas Müller:	It could have, but...

Justin Allen:	My only point is…that painting a picture of it, like a diagram of it. It could be the case that there's you, Andreas. What you're saying is, "After I died, then I could be Andreas." The authentic, natural Andreas. Whereas, before, you were being an in-authentic, unnatural Andreas because you had this seeking energy taking over, in a way.
Andreas Müller:	Yeah, one could say so. But as that, I of course was also 100% authentic.
Justin Allen:	Yeah, you were authentic in believing that this is…
Andreas Müller:	In being a seeker and, in all this apparent inauthenticity, I was authentic.
Justin Allen:	Yeah. But it's like a computer is kind of like blank hardware. And then you put software in it, and then that software makes it act and do certain things that it might not do otherwise. Or you program it with one type of software, and then at some point somebody pushes in another software and that other software overrides the initial software and makes it go against its original software.
Andreas Müller:	Yeah, kind of. One could say so. Of course, all of that isn't real. But that would be in the story. One could see it like that.
Justin Allen:	So in that sense, this is the kind of sales point from available teachings. Like spiritual self-help type teachings, that's the attractive sales pitch in a way. It's still similar to that. The idea that you're there and there's an ego and all you have to do is let go of the ego, then you can be free and be yourself finally. Or like the famous Hollywood movie where somebody is following a life and then something happens and they can then go and do what they wanted to do all along.

Andreas Müller:	And then, finally, they start painting and are very happy and fulfilled because they started painting. That's the personal idea.
Justin Allen:	So, the "me," the way that you've described it and Tony have described it, is that it's a contraction or an energetic...nobody knows what's happening. You're telling a story when you go this way. And the story is that, somehow, there's a person, meaning just a physical person, and then somehow it gets overridden by a sense of me.
Andreas Müller:	Yeah. In a way, that's actually what people report. That's what the "me" reports about itself.
Justin Allen:	Everybody has a first memory or a first sense of when I was there. For me, I wouldn't say I felt like I was there when I was three because I don't have a memory of being three. But whatever it is, that's when Justin started.
Andreas Müller:	Yeah.
Justin Allen:	And so then you're stuck in that. Whatever it wants to do is what you think you're doing. You think that your "me" has to go in this direction. A "me" could be that they want to earn a lot of money, seeking that way. And then it could be seeking a family or seeking spirituality or all this. If that were to end for some people, it could be that they still seek money afterward. It could be that their initial seeking energy...
Andreas Müller:	That's hard to say. Not really, because, of course, when the person seeks, it's always to fulfill this inner lack, to fulfill this need. But I know what you mean. I mean, there's the possibility that you just stay in your job and make the same amount of money as you did before. That's possible. But not really because you seek it.

Justin Allen:

I don't mean that the intention is the same. I just mean that it could also be that the path that you were on is actually the path that you stay on. On paper, like how it looks from the outside.

Andreas Müller:

Oh, kind of, yeah, you could have maybe a career and you just climb up the career ladder or something.

Justin Allen:

Either way, you're starting off like nothing. And then, at some point, you make a claim like you're something. And as soon as that claim happens that you're something, then you need to do something, also.

Andreas Müller:

About oneself. That's the thing. Because it feels instantly unfulfilling.

Justin Allen:

Yeah.

Andreas Müller:

So instantly there will be a seeking or finding a solution to that. Coming out of it. Automatically.

Justin Allen:

And that's something that you've talked about a lot of times. I would be interested in trying to define that a little bit. I feel like I've acknowledged this before, but right now I'm not able to, this having a separation? Why does it necessarily mean dissatisfaction?

Andreas Müller:

I don't know. There is no answer to this, really. It's just what seems to be happening. I know this doesn't make sense. This is so spongy. (laughs)

Justin Allen:

I felt like you have given answers to that.

Andreas Müller:

No, not really. I mean, all those answers would be stories because, of course, it's not true that there is a separate energy that is unfulfilled.

Justin Allen:	Right. But even if it is true, why does separation necessitate dissatisfaction?
Andreas Müller:	In the end, it doesn't. But, it's just what seems to be happening.
Justin Allen:	Because in this sense, you're just saying that the dissatisfaction isn't a dissatisfaction.
Andreas Müller:	Well, no, I mean, it's just what seems to be happening, that everyone who feels that they are someone is seeking in one way or the other.
Justin Allen:	Yeah, but that doesn't have the word "dissatisfaction."
Andreas Müller:	Well, yeah. To me, seeking and dissatisfaction go together. Because without this dissatisfaction, there wouldn't be seeking. So it's a very instantaneous reaction to dissatisfaction, the seeking. And quite in the moment, you know, not "I'm seeking in money" or something. I mean, the seeker, from moment to moment, tries to find an answer to this instantaneous dissatisfaction. So, to say people seek money, that's already a very simplified and broad story. So even the people who seek money, actually, in every moment they feel they are, they need to find an answer to this present moment. Tell themselves a story about why they couldn't... it's much more instantaneous to seeking, actually.
Justin Allen:	People have created a lot of stories about...that man and woman come from the same sex or something like that. It's some kind of folklore or something that everybody's born almost sexless in a way. Then, when they become physical, they take on a gender. And they have to find their mate to reunite again. It's the same thing as "My true love is out there somewhere, I just have to find her or find him." But in this case, it's somehow making

it very related to the fact that we're just one. And then, somehow, we get born as two. And then, to have that sense of wholeness or union again, we have to find our match again. And then we also, in a sense, lose our gender again. That's a story that explains why it is that you feel like you have to seek out a mate. Why you feel happy and great when you find somebody that you feel compatible with? But in your case, there's no explanation as to why there's dissatisfaction. You're just saying there seems to be dissatisfaction when there's separation.

Andreas Müller: Yeah, exactly. And also, I don't mean it as a teaching or general knowledge or something. It's useless to know that. And in the end, it's irrelevant if it is like that or not in a broader sense. Because, in a way, this conversation, or what happens in the meetings, is a very direct reply to the energy that's going on there. The more we talk about the world and how it generally is, every me is seeking and stuff. I mean, that's all stories that are unknown in the end.

Justin Allen: I started by saying that I recall the time when you said, "When I died being a "me," then I could finally be me." And in that storyline, it's kind of implied that seeking means separation and dissatisfaction. They're all simultaneously...

Andreas Müller: Exactly. They are all the same dynamic.

Justin Allen: So, when that died, then that dissatisfaction and seeking wasn't there anymore.

Andreas Müller: Yeah.

Justin Allen: So it seems like the separation, in your case, is saying that initially you're whole. Or, in actuality, you're whole. But there's some kind of an illusion that you're not whole.

Andreas Müller: Yup.

Justin Allen: And then as soon as that happens, it's kind of like you want to be whole again.

Andreas Müller: Kind of, yeah.

Justin Allen: Without knowing it because you don't know what that means, but whatever the seeking means, even if it's money or family or whatever; essentially, you're trying to seek wholeness through those things.

Andreas Müller: Kind of. The person doesn't really seek wholeness. It seeks an experience of what it thinks wholeness would be. Or at least it tries to get rid of the dissatisfaction and thinks, "If I get rid of the dissatisfaction, I will have a fulfilled experience."

Justin Allen: Even though this is also meaningless, just as a way to try to create a diagram or a vision of it, what came to my mind was thinking about a loaf of bread. It's a whole loaf of bread. And if you took a piece of that bread away and set it over one meter away from the loaf of bread, that thing (crumb) might feel like it's separated and wants to get back to the whole (loaf). Right?

Andreas Müller: (laughs) Yeah, that's a very sweet picture, to be honest. Maybe after this book, we can make a children's book with a piece of bread that wants to... yeah.

Justin Allen: Or, spiritual teachers use the ocean, right?

Andreas Müller: Yeah, the ocean and the wave thing.

Justin Allen: Yeah, the ocean and the wave thing. That's the same in a way of the crumb from the loaf of bread being separated.

Andreas Müller:	Yeah.
Justin Allen:	I mean, the wave one's better than the bread one. (laughs)
Andreas Müller:	Well, I like the bread one too.
Justin Allen:	The bread one gets away from it. And then in my mind I immediately go, if it was separated, why would it want to go back?
Andreas Müller:	Yeah, then it's free. (laughs) It could just walk off.
Justin Allen:	Exactly.
Andreas Müller:	And enjoy it.
Justin Allen:	But the ocean one's good because it never actually separates from the ocean.
Andreas Müller:	The thing is, what does all of that imply? What's the conclusion?
Justin Allen:	With the ocean one, it implies that there isn't separation.
Andreas Müller:	Exactly.
Justin Allen:	But it implies that when you think that you're separated if all there is, is ocean, but somehow the wave or the crest identifies as being separate. Even that, it doesn't answer the question: why is it bad to feel like you're the white part of the ocean?
Andreas Müller:	Yeah. There is no answer to that.
Justin Allen:	Yeah, that's true. That whole story, then, is just a clever story to make you feel...
Andreas Müller:	To give you, again, a kind of an answer.

Justin Allen: Yeah.

Andreas Müller: To give you some kind of comfort.

Justin Allen: Because everybody is comfortable with that. If we
                       did write a children's book of a loaf of bread, and
                       then a crumb fell away and that crumb was like, oh
                       no...

Andreas Müller: Oh no, I'm...

Justin Allen: I'm... lost. I'm away from my mom and dad. How do
                       I get back to it? Everybody would accept that 100%.

Andreas Müller: 100%. Absolutely.

Justin Allen: They would accept that it's dissatisfied and wants
                       to return to the bread.

Andreas Müller: That's true, actually. Yeah, you're right. Yeah, it
                       would just be accepted.

Justin Allen: Without questioning, like, why is it dissatisfied?

Andreas Müller: Yeah, exactly. They wouldn't be like, "What? You
                       are free now. Be just a small breadcrumb sepa-
                       rate from the prison of the mother bread." (laughs)
                       Yeah.

Justin Allen: People do accept that they're alone. Most people,
                       a lot of it is, is like people feeling alone and feeling
                       like they need to connect and be with somebody
                       else also.

Andreas Müller: Yeah. Connect to something. I don't know if it nec-
                       essarily has to be a partner.

Justin Allen: Well, I'm just saying the fact is that the majority of
                       people seek out partners and spend a lot of mon-
                       ey and time seeking them out as well. And there's

even a pressure on it and feeling like you're worth-less if you don't have a partner.

Andreas Müller: I get it, yeah. That's a huge issue for many people. For most people, I guess.

Justin Allen: Well, that's interesting in a way that there's no answer for this.

Andreas Müller: I mean, the dissatisfaction is dreamt, but that's not the answer to it. In a way, the person's problem is that there is no answer to their dissatisfaction.

Justin Allen: Why are they dissatisfied with not having an answer? That's already another form of separation. Thinking that there has to be an answer is also like...that you have to be with this loaf of bread.

Andreas Müller: Yeah, absolutely. I have no answer. For no reason. And all I say is just useless. The person can't just do anything with it. Then I would say it's all wholeness. It's what seems to be happening for no reason. But it doesn't make sense. There is no answer. People walking around thinking they are someone being dissatisfied doesn't make sense. It's not a logical thing that comes out of, "Oh yeah, okay, that's why I decided...mmm, yeah, true. That makes sense. It's okay to feel dissatisfied because it's caused by this, and it's..." It's not real at all. It's not based on any reality. It's not based on any "It has to be like that because..." No, not at all. To be "me" and dis-satisfied doesn't make sense at all. I mean, Nothing makes sense, but this, too, doesn't make sense. And I don't have an answer to that at all. I can't explain it. I don't know why it happens. I don't know where it's coming from. It's just what seems to be happening.

Justin Allen: I always thought that you guys had some kind of an answer for that.

Andreas Müller: No, I'm sorry. Ha!

Justin Allen: But even that is evidence that...somehow I've listened to a certain amount of this. And I just kind of, in my head, assumed that there was an answer to it. Everybody starts off somehow saying, "At some point, the contraction happens, you know? You don't accept that. At least, I don't. I always think, what the fuck does that mean, anyway? What does a contraction mean? That's also answerless.

Andreas Müller: Well, the sense of "I am."

Justin Allen: I know, but it's, why do you call it a contraction?

Andreas Müller: Oh, I think Tony called it because it just feels like that: "I'm a me."

Justin Allen: He's inventing a word to try to...

Andreas Müller: Again, it's the me describing it's own, experience. I'm "me." I'm present. I'm something. I feel tense, I feel burdened by the world, and I feel kind of contracted.

Justin Allen: It's just a total story. But when you hear it; it's the same way as when Mom and Dad say Santa comes down the chimney and delivers presents. You just accept it.

Andreas Müller: Yeah, I think in this case, it's a little bit different because, of course, the person accepts the story. But the person also recognizes their own experience in that. So, it's not just accepting a random story. It kind of is because it just is a story, but it also points to its own experience. I think that's why the breadcrumb story is instantly accepted, that this single breadcrumb is suffering from being separated because it also is the person's experience. It's not just a story that the person believes in, that I'm suffering. In a very funny way, it also feels like that. That's why there is this instant connection to this story.

Justin Allen: I'm just saying that when you hear it, you just accept it. Also, when you hear one of you guys say, "And then there's separation," you skip over, "Why is separation bad, and why does it cause you to want to become unseparated," in a sense? But the separation is just saying that something's there now. Because if you answered that kind of question or you followed that kind of path, saying at some point it seems to be that something's there. Or something claiming to be there. And as soon as that happens, then there seems to be a desire or some energy that says, I don't want to be here anymore, or I want to...

Andreas Müller: Be here in a better way. Enlightened. Happy. Fulfilled. More money. Yeah, that's what seems to be happening.

Justin Allen: And then you also talk about the reality of that longing that somebody has, right? In that one case, maybe it's to have a better experience, right?

Andreas Müller: In the end, it's always to have a better experience. That's the only thing the person can imagine or seek for; with various stories, so to speak. But it's always only to have a better experience.

Justin Allen: I think that Jim Newman differentiates that a little bit. Somehow there's a difference between him saying that there's a longing. He says something about what you're longing for, even though you don't know, is freedom. And what he means by that is the "no me."

Andreas Müller: But my impression is that the person will always translate this longing into having a better experience.

Justin Allen: But ultimately, they don't want to be there anymore. The ultimate thing is that they don't want to "be" anymore.

Andreas Müller: Yes and no. I don't see it like that because no one wants to be dead. But I understand this longing for total peace, in the end, is the longing to be absent.

Justin Allen: But nobody wants that.

Andreas Müller: Whenever there is a person, there is longing; that's how I see it is translated into: I'll have a better experience.

Justin Allen: It's not possible that somebody could long for their absence.

Andreas Müller: Exactly.

Justin Allen: So they have to make it something that they can imagine.

Andreas Müller: Imagine. And, of course, a lot of people imagine absence to be something and say, "I want to get rid of me," or stuff like that. But what they're actually still imagining is some kind of an experience. But I understand. I mean, one could say this whole... people coming to these meetings. In a way, they long for something else, apparently. But in their story, until the end, as long as they are someone, what they are looking for is a better experience.

                        But I understand. It's not the "me" that brings people to these meetings. So, in that sense, one could say those two things are going: the longing for something else than being a "me," but the "me" still thinks, until the end, it's about me having a better experience.

Justin Allen: But generally, in that context, somebody that listens to your talks for the first time, let's say, could come to your talks and also could hear you and think that they're hearing something similar to a spiritual teacher.

Andreas Müller: Oh yeah.

Justin Allen: If they've only been listening to spiritual teachers or if maybe you're the first time they decide, "I want to go to a spiritual teacher" and somebody says, "Go to Andreas Müller."

Andreas Müller: Yes.

Justin Allen: They're probably still going to interpret you in the context of you teaching something and...

Andreas Müller: Absolutely. And this also happens to people, even those who understand that it's not a spiritual teaching. They still think it's some kind of teaching that will bring them a fulfilling experience. But some people just manage to keep up the idea that I'm just using a different language than spiritual teachers.

Justin Allen: Yeah, but there are a lot of people also that...they go to your meeting, even understanding that you're not a spiritual teacher, not expecting that you're going to solve anything for them.

Andreas Müller: Yes and no. Because as I said, as long as there is someone, there is some kind of hope of some kind of deeper resolution.

Justin Allen: But they could still be under the impression that it's as likely that a change is going to happen listening to you as when they're cooking in their kitchen.

Andreas Müller: Absolutely.

Justin Allen:

So for them, it could be that they're just going to spend time with you and listen to you the same way that they're going to cook a meal, or that they're going to talk with a friend.

Andreas Müller:

Kind of, one could say so. I think for most people who have been with this message for a while, it's energetically quite obvious if there is someone teaching something. Because the enjoyment is that there is no one teaching something. That's the energy of freedom around this message. And, of course, most people get pushed away even if someone tries to teach them. But there are a few people who manage to go on thinking that this is a teaching. Some people tell me "other teachers," as an example, "They are good. They describe it in a good way. With you, I don't understand it, but that's very clear how Rupert says it," or something.

Justin Allen:

Yeah.

Andreas Müller:

I have no idea how this is possible actually, but it happens.

Justin Allen:

So, I'm not going to be that good at talking about it, but I'll just follow it to see if it leads to something. How aware are you of the Schrödinger cat dilemma?

Andreas Müller:

Ah, yeah, it's this, is it dead already or alive thing? Yeah, not deeply.

Justin Allen:

I'm not either. Maybe a little bit, (laughs) just a little bit more than you.

Andreas Müller:

(laughs) That's a good basis for having a deep conversation on it.

Justin Allen:

And what about quantum mechanics?

Andreas Müller:	(laughs) Well, I think the problem with Schrödinger's Cat is that there is still someone left who doesn't know; that there is someone who can't say if it's either or.
Justin Allen:	It's used to explain the dilemma of things that they can't prove yet related to quantum mechanics where there's...right now there's, let's say, four arguments that try to explain what's happening, but each are flawed and not provable.
Andreas Müller:	Yeah, but that's basically what I mean. There's still someone left who just doesn't know. Could be this, could be like this, could be like this, but I don't know which way it is; but subtly still assuming it will be one way.
Justin Allen:	Maybe, but there's also...somebody has a multiverse theory, which says that...
Andreas Müller:	Which would still be in one way, which means that there are three options simultaneously. The case which may not be logical to the "me," but the "me" would still say, "Okay, maybe it is like that. I just can't get it."
Justin Allen:	What do you know about quantum mechanics?
Andreas Müller:	(laughs) Hardly anything, I'd say.
Justin Allen:	But do you know where it is, in the hierarchy of sciences?
Andreas Müller:	No.
Justin Allen:	I might also be wrong with what I'm saying, but I think that it's the new science. It's limited because physics doesn't take into consideration even smaller particles, and then quantum now tries to take the smallest particles that we're aware of.

| Andreas Müller: | They're approaching the truth, so to speak. |

| Justin Allen: | Not necessarily that, but it's because of new findings in science that... the rules or the laws that we have, they see don't work, or they can't meet the new findings that they've discovered. Have you ever seen that experiment where they have a piece of paper, and it has two slits in it, and then behind is another piece of paper, and then they shoot electrons through it? And then electrons, now, they say are particles and waves simultaneously. And because of that, I think what happens sometimes is that they go through (the slits) and then there should be a line of light here and a line of light here. And the particles that go through this side of the slit, should be over here. But they end up over here. |

| Andreas Müller: | Yeah. |

| Justin Allen: | And they can't say where one particle is going to go. They can't tell you beforehand that it's going to end up here. All they can do is give the probability that it'll be in this general location in a way. But the thing that's perplexing to them is that it is evidence that things can be in two places at once and that you can't predetermine or find out where something is (or is going to be). And as soon as you measure it, it loses its value, or it loses its previous reality. And that has something to do with the Schrödinger cat experiment, that when you open the box, it will be shown (the cat) as either dead or alive, but until (you open the box) you can't determine what it is. So it's either alive or dead, or it's both alive and dead. But when you open the box, it's going to be one or the other, even though before that, it could have been either or. When I read that, the way that I relate it to this (message) is that science seems to be going in the direction (of this message) more and more... |

Andreas Müller: That's what I meant when I said they are approaching the truth. They seem to come closer to...

Justin Allen: They come closer. But as they come closer, it seems to be that they can't make claims of knowing anymore. Like they seem to be in a direction that's undefinable or that it's...or even that something can be in two places at once, or these ideas mean that they can't prove things and that there isn't one answer, that there isn't one beginning, or things can be dead and alive. So if things can be dead and alive, then it takes away the meaning of being dead and alive, or that you can't say something's dead or alive.

Andreas Müller: Yeah.

Justin Allen: I read a book by Michio Kaku because quantum computing is supposed to take over digital computing; now, or in the next five or 10 years, it's supposed to replace all digital computers. Digital computing uses ones and zeros as bits, and then they give this example to try to understand it. There's a maze here, and the maze has 10 paths that are possible. The digital computer has to try out each 10 paths and then it'll tell you the right way to go. Quantum computing can, because it's computing at a molecular level, whereas a digital computer uses bits of ones and zeros. Because it's at the atomic level or whatever. (laughs) It can simultaneously all at once, test all the paths; just, in a diagrammatic way, it can test every path all at once and know the answer all at once without having to go through each step.

Andreas Müller: Yeah. Okay.

Justin Allen: And they don't know why it can do that. They just know that it's doing that.

Andreas Müller: (laughs) That's great.

Justin Allen: Another thing they talk about is that now they will introduce quantum computing with AI and the possibilities of the data they can get will far surpass everything. When I read it, I just can't help but find correlations with the message of not being here either. And also with consciousness, they question even the reality that we're conscious. Seems like all leading scientists that that's no longer a...

Andreas Müller: It's amazing because that's basically what this message is saying in the end. But, there are no words for this, but coming from this directness. Yeah. There is nothing real. There is no consciousness, and automatically nothing is real anymore. And everything is simultaneously everything and nothing at the same time, but for no one. And everything is possible, and nothing is possible. So, that's just how it is. But they are still dancing around it.

Justin Allen: Sort of, but that's what I was trying to find before I came here. I was reading a bit about Schrödinger and seeing if I would be able to paraphrase, but I couldn't. I didn't find something I could grab onto. But when I read these books and hear talks and the new experiments and discoveries and stuff like that, it always seems to have a healthy relationship with this message that you have with the other people as well. It's interesting.

Andreas Müller: It's very funny that, in a way, they know less and less in the end.

Justin Allen: Or that they know more and more, but the discovery of knowing more is indicating that there's not (anything to know)...

Andreas Müller: Yeah.

Justin Allen: They have these principles, and one is called the uncertainty principle, and that has something to do with quantum mechanics. It has something to do with the fact that there seems to be a law that there can't be a law. It's like a paradoxical thing that there's an element of randomness that is provable in a way, even though you can't prove it. Also, if you say the sentences, everything's nothing, and Nothing's everything, there are sentences like that that are coming out of science.

Andreas Müller: Yeah. I found it funny that I think it was neuroscientists or something; I don't know the numbers anymore, but they assume now that 90 percent of the thoughts are following patterns, and are predictable. And that there are 10 percent or a small percentage of thoughts, which are just random and can't be predicted at all. (laughs) Which I liked very much, because in the end this explains very much how life is quite orderly, but in a very unpredictable way, at some point, something else happens which you haven't foreseen; which hasn't been predictable. So it's like a hundred times the person does the same thing, but one time it's just slightly different and you never know. So it explains this, and it explains nothing.

Justin Allen: You know how, at least anecdotally, you've heard about artists, musicians, or painters who write some very famous song, and then somebody asks them in an interview, "How did you come up with the song?" And...

Andreas Müller: "It came to me" or something.

Justin Allen: Yeah, or that they don't feel like they can take credit for it.

Andreas Müller: Yeah.

Justin Allen: I feel that way, also. Nobody's ever come to me to give me accolades of (laughs) success, like Bob Dylan, you know? Nobody's coming to me saying how great I am at something. But if someone were to put all this prestige on me and say, "Wow, look at what you've accomplished" or "Look at what you've done," I wouldn't feel like I did it.

Andreas Müller: Mm-Hmm, yeah, of course.

Justin Allen: And if I was supposed to go, yeah, I'm the one that invented this and I want to reap all the rewards and take all the credit for it, it wouldn't feel right. At least I would never believe that I did it.

Andreas Müller: Yeah. But maybe you would entertain the idea that it happened to you.

Justin Allen: That the idea happened to me?

Andreas Müller: Or the talent you have, or...

Justin Allen: Even that, I wouldn't. I would want to say something like it seems obvious to me that I'm the one who's getting credit for it and that it's somehow coming out of me. I would only say that from the external world. If I'm the one that makes something and this is an invention, then the world is going to think I did it; but I wouldn't feel like I did it.

Andreas Müller: Yeah.

Justin Allen: When you were you before and you had an idea or you wrote something, you felt like you were writing it.

Andreas Müller: Yeah. I mean, it's always a mixture of things. Probably I would've said that the idea came to me, but I wrote it down.

Justin Allen: But then the next step would be that you didn't choose to write it down either.

Andreas Müller:	Both don't happen. Things don't happen to anyone and there's no one doing anything.

Justin Allen:	So in that case the idea didn't come to you and there was no you to execute the idea.

Andreas Müller:	Exactly. This you is dreamt; the observer and the doer.

Justin Allen:	My reason for bringing this up is that, don't you think that a lot of people think that way? Or do you think that people genuinely think that they're the ones that have the idea, and they're the ones that are manifesting the idea?

Andreas Müller:	Yeah, both. I think the "me" can either have the impression that things happen to it or that it's doing things. Mostly, it's a mixture of all of it. But I think there are a lot of people who think that it's because of them that they have great ideas and that they write great poetry because there is a "me" who can do that. You'll find both. You'll find a lot of people who feel almost guilty for being admired because they notice that, "Well, I didn't do it, but it happened to (me)."

Justin Allen:	It's more like a shame, too.

Andreas Müller:	Exactly. But others can say it's okay that I'm admired because it came to me. It's not me doing it, but life gave it to me. This ability or this talent. So it's always either the experiencer or the doer, and both can be experienced as good or as bad. That's why I think you can find all of it in people.

Justin Allen:	But when you're giving a talk or writing a book, you are saying, in a sense, whatever seems to be coming out of my writing or out of my talks isn't coming from me, and there's nothing they're choosing; that they're (I'm) going to say this or that.

Andreas Müller: Exactly. And it's also not happening to me or through me.

Justin Allen: You're not some vessel. You're not a computer that somebody's putting software into.

Andreas Müller: Exactly, yeah.

Justin Allen: And you don't think that the majority of people think that way. Do you think the majority of the people think that it's their idea and they're the ones executing the idea?

Andreas Müller: No, I don't say that. I think it's just quite random. But it will either be: it happens to me, or I'm doing it.

Justin Allen: Or both.

Andreas Müller: Or both. For most people, it's always a mix. Their personal experience is always a mix of things that happen to them and things that they can choose or do. I think that's quite common. The personal experience is quite common, and then it somehow subtly feels like that. But of course, I guess some people don't think about it at all; "Is this happening to me?" or "I'm doing this?" or... but I think this would be the impression when there is someone.

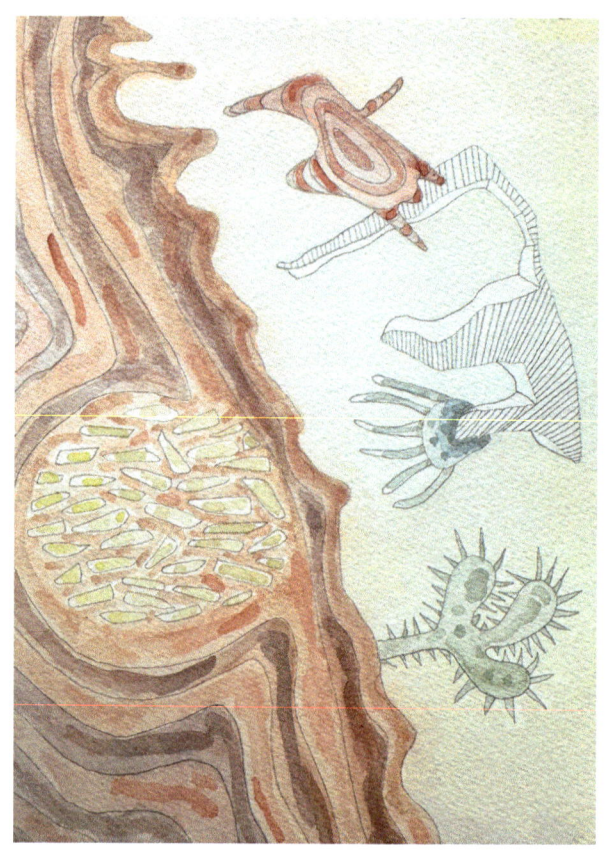

BREAD LOAF

Justin Allen: I walked around your village today and thought I would just paint a picture of where you are. You're in a small village with a main street and an intersection with three-story high buildings at the corner. And then you have a bakery, a pharmacy, an Italian restaurant not run by Italians. And then a Chinese, Indian, Pizza, American hamburger all-in-one run by Sikhs. Hairdressers, and then an Edeka supermarket chain. I walked along a little creek, and there were tennis courts, a football field, and volleyball (courts). And there's a new building there, a sports hall. When you look out your window, you're on the top floor. You can see rolling hills and pastures. It looks like a gentleman's farm. Just a beautiful piece of property that is manicured, so it's just a normal German village 30 minutes outside of Stuttgart. I wanted to point out just in case somebody has the idea that you're a guru. This isn't... (laughs)

Andreas Müller: (laughs) Living in my castle in the most gorgeous...

Justin Allen: This isn't a guru setting. If I put it from an American perspective, it would be like going to a small town in upstate New York where there's a supermarket, a main street, a post office, some cafes, a couple of restaurants, and most of the people that work there work in a city that might be 30 minutes away. It's not a town that would necessarily be on a postcard or that they would want to shoot a movie in or anything like that.

Andreas Müller:	Yeah.
Justin Allen:	So it's just average and nice.
Andreas Müller:	Yeah, exactly.
Justin Allen:	And then your apartment itself, you're on the top floor, which is nice. You have a balcony. Then you have a little kitchenette. It's not big, and it's almost small.
Andreas Müller:	Yeah.
Justin Allen:	And then you have an okay-sized living room. Probably, you're in 60 square meters. So, 600 square feet. And then you have a bedroom and a bathroom. And then I would guess your furniture is mostly Ikea.
Andreas Müller:	That's true, yeah. (laughs)
Justin Allen:	And you have a couple of paintings on the wall. You have a small library. But if I walked into this apartment without knowing you, I would not assume at all that you're into spirituality or that you are a guru-type person.
Andreas Müller:	It's just ordinary. You might have noticed there's a small corner of non-duality books (laughs) on my bookshelf, but...
Justin Allen:	Just looking at it for one second, I saw the Bible. I saw something that looks like a guru-type book, like Osho or...
Andreas Müller:	Yeah, something like that. But the Bible it's from school.
Justin Allen:	Everybody's library has at least one or two spiritual books anyway.

Andreas Müller:	Up there, there are Tony's books, but not too many.
Justin Allen:	If somebody had a romantic vision about wanting to come here to meet you, thinking that they're going to get some kind of mystical, spiritual experience, this won't meet their expectations. (laughs)
Andreas Müller:	(laughs) Thank you. It's just ordinary. I feel very at home here.
Justin Allen:	When I was 20, I had an idea of being enlightened, and I was aware of some people; I was aware of Krishnamurti, but he was in Ojai, California. It's a village up in the mountains, and it has a nice name and nice nature.
Andreas Müller:	I've been there once, I'd given talks there.
Justin Allen:	So you know what it's like. And then he seemed like he lived on a farm that was paid from somebody that sponsored his message or teachings, or if you think of…that you have to go to an ashram to get enlightened and that has a certain romantic expectation or appeal that you're gonna go… In the minds of people my age and my generation plus or minus 20 years, probably if they're interested in becoming enlightened, in whatever form that is, and they think that they need somebody to get them there. The person that they think will help them get there, I'm sure that they're imagining that you have to go through some kind of struggle to get there. It's not that easy. It's in some kind of very rural setting, or if it was in an urban setting, that it would somehow be detached a bit, like a monastery or something.
Andreas Müller:	Or something. (laughs)
Justin Allen:	And that it would be very hard to meet this person that you want to meet so badly (desperately), and maybe they would give you one hour of their time after you struggled for two weeks to get there and

spent however much money. (laughs) And then the person would come out with blue eyes and be some kind of vision of what you think is ideal or somebody that's...

Andreas Müller: Maybe even an entourage or something like that.

Justin Allen: And then they would give you some little bit of wisdom or what you think of as being wisdom, and then you would feel maybe like you've figured something out. And this isn't like that in the sense that here you can just take a plane or a train to Stuttgart

Andreas Müller: From the airport, it would take 15 minutes.

Justin Allen: And then you're never for one moment detached from society or reality or technology or all the normal services. And then you can stay here in this town in an average hotel. And then, if you were open to it, people could meet with you.

Andreas Müller: Oh yeah, absolutely. Of course.

Justin Allen: Realistically, it'd be like if it's in New York State, or around Berlin, and you have a friend or a sister or brother that lives nearby, it's almost like that. It'd be like going to their place, and then saying, "Hey, let's go have a coffee." And then you talk for two hours and then you say bye and then even maybe return in the evening, like we're doing right now and having a conversation and that's it.

Andreas Müller: Yep.

Justin Allen: Totally normal.

Andreas Müller: Totally. Of course.

Justin Allen: The 20-year-old me, if somehow I would have met you under these circumstances, I feel like I would have been disappointed, and it would have played into my ideas of what enlightenment should be. I would have felt ripped off. This isn't what I imagined, and this isn't...what's this gonna do? This is just like meeting a friend.

Andreas Müller: Exactly. What's this about? There's nothing. There's nothing special. There's nothing to get, really. Yeah.

Justin Allen: And now I don't have that because I've talked with you a couple of times. I don't even have that idea or that mental image in my mind anymore. So I just wanted to point out that it's just sitting here, like I'm talking to a friend or even my father or a sibling. It's that low-key and easy.

Andreas Müller: That's just how it is. The surprise is that the natural reality is ordinary; that it is this, and not something special.

Justin Allen: I would still imagine that it's a majority that would come to you, at least initially. They would probably have the impression that enlightenment is something else other than what happens here.

Andreas Müller: Absolutely.

Justin Allen: That can also be a big disappointment and even a hurdle for them to meet with you on an ordinary, low-key level. Because even though you might be there all the time on an ordinary, low-key, relaxed level, people have their projections and ideas in their head that give them a much different perspective of what's happening in a meeting with you.

Andreas Müller: Oh, totally, of course. But, surprisingly, I'd say most people aren't disappointed. I mean, people who are interested in this message or who do meet me in a meeting or in this context, of course, look for something special because that's what the person does anyway. And I think most people are, on the one hand, disappointed. But on the other hand, the flavor of this message is also there. The flavor of the freedom of not getting anything. So it's not really getting less than expected. Then, it would be only disappointing. It's kind of getting nothing, but at the same time, maybe tasting a kind of freedom that's in that.

Justin Allen: Yeah, I agree.

Andreas Müller: But the expectations or the pictures that the person has about what this is about or how it will be or how I am or... those will, of course, be disappointed or (laughs) destroyed.

Justin Allen: I can still imagine, even for those people that are confronted with the ordinariness of yourself and the ordinariness of the message, even the environments in which you teach are also without bells and whistles. I would imagine that, if they're listening to you for two hours, there's some hurdle for them to accept; that this isn't what I was expecting. If somebody's going to your meeting with a preconceived notion that they're going to be meeting somebody, that's going to help them get enlightened. And then that person comes in wearing jeans and a shirt and not sitting with perfect posture, and they're pretending like they're very aware and present in the moment; that it can be a hurdle for them to accept...

Andreas Müller: Oh, totally. Absolutely. Most people wouldn't come here. I mean, most spiritual people just aren't interested in this message, and also, in the presentation of this message, because it's too ordinary. Of course. They wouldn't even acknowledge it at some point. They look for something special and one could almost say, especially, spiritual seekers look for something very special.

Justin Allen: And that ties into your message, or at least things I've heard from your message, and also all the others that are in line with your message. There's a sentence that comes out that it's so obvious that you miss it.

Andreas Müller: Mm hmm.

Justin Allen: I always think that that statement's a little bit loaded because it means, "Oh, I'm so stupid. All these years, I was..."

Andreas Müller: You actually don't hear that from me.

Justin Allen: But you know what I'm saying.

Andreas Müller: Yeah...

Justin Allen: If, let's just pretend that your message is the only, I don't want to say, true message, but it's the only one that has some kind of I don't know, I can't finish the sentence without incriminating you.

Andreas Müller: Yeah, we can't go there. It's so difficult. But it's the only in-person message or message that, apparently, really points to something that's not personal.

Justin Allen: The presentation is ordinary. Generally, all the people that I've seen that have this message also seem...Tony Parsons seems a little bit...not like he's a guru, but just because he has a certain status because of his age, maybe, and he dresses a little bit sharp. It doesn't have to do with anything guru, but he draws a larger audience.

Andreas Müller: I think this may give that impression sometimes.

Justin Allen: But he still comes off as a normal, regular guy.

Andreas Müller: Absolutely.

Justin Allen:

And because of that, because of the presentation, that the presentation is so ordinary, that the person with the message is so ordinary, and then also because of the crowd. Even if they're expecting a guru within 30 minutes or an hour or a couple of meetings, they generally drop that expectation and have had a taste of the message and are kind of excited about it or interested or...

Andreas Müller:

Yeah, I think so. It's quite amazing how quickly, in a meeting, this energy takes over. All those superficial or appearance details don't matter anymore, really. How I am, how I look, what I do. Is it ordinary or not?

Justin Allen:

If you're going to any kind of retreat that you can, and you go from a well-known, accepted teacher guru type person, and then you come to your meeting, there will be the person that says, "What the fuck is this? This has nothing to do with spirituality. This is total bullshit." And then they go back to the...

Andreas Müller:

Spiritual guru.

Justin Allen:

The one with a nice presentation, the one that somehow looks special, and has some kind of an entourage maybe, and they have all the bells and whistles. And because they have all the bells and whistles, usually we're drawn to that and expect a bigger reward from that. Whereas your message has no bells and whistles and you as a person don't have bells and whistles and the message also doesn't. It's more or less like one or two sentences that just... you can talk about them in thousands of different ways like you can with anything. It's a simple, basic message, and it's delivered in a very simple, straightforward way, also.

Andreas Müller:	I think it can only be that way. Naturally. It's not made. It's not an artificial ordinariness or something. That's just how I am and that's just how this is. And I don't see how it can be otherwise.
Justin Allen:	There would be differences of course. Let's say, a kind of intellectual professor type person was liberated and the "me" died for that person. But that person had taught in university for 40 years, and that person will sound different explaining this message than you will.
Andreas Müller:	Of course, but my impression is it would just still be ordinary.
Justin Allen:	It's just plain talk. (laughs)
Andreas Müller:	Exactly, it just wouldn't be, those bells and whistles, as they say.
Justin Allen:	I was thinking about us talking about separation, and why separation breeds discontent.
Andreas Müller:	There's a sense of dissatisfaction. I like that. That seems to go together.
Justin Allen:	Why is there this dissatisfaction? We said we don't know. There's no answer to why that automatically means dissatisfaction. What if you started off (as) separated? You were separated, and you were forced into wholeness, let's say. You couldn't then be dissatisfied because there's no longer a "you" there to be dissatisfied. When you're separated, then there's a point of view or a frame of reference. Even if we take that loaf of bread: if all there is, is a loaf of bread and there's nothing else, it's just that, and you pull a piece out, now you've created two things. That thing that you pulled out is insubstantial because it's not a part of the whole anymore. So now it's its own thing. But if you started off that

way, as ist (your) own thing, and that's all you knew, and then that crumb was put back into the loaf of bread, (laughs) it wouldn't have any sense of identity anymore. It couldn't claim anything.

Andreas Müller: Exactly.

Justin Allen: It couldn't say, "I wish that I was separated again," because it's not there to wish that it was separated anymore.

Andreas Müller: Exactly. Absolutely. And actually, that's the personal experience. The personal experience starts off being the separate part. The person never knows wholeness or that it has been whole. All it knows is, "I'm separate."

Justin Allen: At that moment, Yeah.

Andreas Müller: That's actually the starting point, always, for the person.

Justin Allen: So if you have the loaf of bread and then you take the crumb away from it, that crumb was there in the loaf of bread.

Andreas Müller: Yeah, but the funny thing is, that crumb doesn't know that. It only knows being separate.

Justin Allen: But it was there because it matches. All the contours of its crust and everything that matches. But now is the first time that it could claim that I'm (it's) something. Whereas before, it couldn't.

Andreas Müller: Exactly.

Justin Allen: Then you could start to understand why it breeds dissatisfaction only because it can. It's also a part of the freedom. It can be dissatisfied because that's a possibility now, whereas before it wouldn't be a possibility.

Andreas Müller:	Absolutely, but in the end, it's still not an explanation. It's just a logical story that you tell to it. Still, it doesn't really answer why.
Justin Allen:	Other than that it can.
Andreas Müller:	I know what you mean, but it's not really an answer to why.
Justin Allen:	It's like an answer of "If it can happen, it will happen, or that it could happen," at least. It almost seems natural that if it's separated, it has the ability to question something.
Andreas Müller:	So to speak. Exactly. That's, what seems to be happening. That's how it seems to be.
Justin Allen:	If you were just born a happy person, unaware, and you're going around the world, and then all of a sudden you meet somebody, and you never once thought about what's the meaning of life, but you meet somebody, and they say, "What's the meaning of life?" And you never thought about it before. Just that question alone could fuck your whole life up in a very superficial way.
Andreas Müller:	Exactly, but also only if you're already living as someone with dissatisfaction.
Justin Allen:	I'm just using a very, very plain pretend scenario.
Andreas Müller:	I got it. I'm just saying that it's not that until then, everything was fine. There was also seeking in some normal ways or what we would regard as normal, having a secure job or whatever. But it would just resonate with something that's already there; a deeper seeking, which is maybe not spiritual and in that sense unconscious. I'm sorry, that's really weird to describe it like that.

Justin Allen: It's like a virus, a little bit. The philosophical question, "Who am I?" it's possible that a human could go through life without any big spiritual dilemma. Like a pretty good life.

Andreas Müller: Yes.

Justin Allen: It could also happen that you go through 20 years of a pretty good life, and then you go to philosophy class, or you hang out with somebody, and somebody says, "Who are you?" All of a sudden, you're like, "Oh shit, who am I? I never thought about that before."

Andreas Müller: (laughs) Yes.

Justin Allen: And then that can send you into a deep rabbit hole of spiritual seeking where, in the beginning, you might be grateful to that person, and then at some point, you could be super angry. It's like they gave you a terrible disease.

Andreas Müller: (laughs) ...invented this problem.

Justin Allen: Exactly. Relating that back to the bread, when that crumb gets pulled away it's almost as if you introduce the question, "Who am I?"

Andreas Müller: Absolutely. Oh, totally.

Justin Allen: And that question, then. Automatically, that question is a dissatisfaction.

Andreas Müller: Exactly. But it's not the question that is the dissatisfaction. The question comes out of that dissatisfaction. And this happens the moment there is separation.

Justin Allen: Yeah, that's what I mean. It's all the same.

Andreas Müller: It's all the same thing. Absolutely.

Justin Allen: You can't say it's the me first, and then the question. You can't say the question first, and then the me. That's one thing. The me is the question, and the question is the me.

Andreas Müller: It's one way to be. Exactly. In that sense, every me is on a spiritual path because every me is looking for something deeper than just the present experience. So even people who...you just made up the story that someone can go through life without any spiritual dilemma still live in a spiritual dilemma because, also, they look for something deeper that they can gain from money or a certain lifestyle. So even those, at least how I see it, are in kind of a spiritual seeking because they look for some meaning or power. I mean, power is also something you can't... it's not really something you can grasp. It's Something in some way. So this would also be a spiritual seeking where the spirit, the me, seeks something deeper than just the plain and ordinary daily experience.

Justin Allen: I thought that was an interesting way to look at it. All these conversations and your conversations always start off that there's just wholeness; that's all there is. But then, somehow, out of this wholeness comes an idea of separation. And the idea of separation is also the seeking and the dissatisfaction and all this. What if it could be reversed? That was an interesting point you said. It gets reversed, and you start off as an individual. And then somebody forces you back into the whole. Or somehow, you are put back into the whole.

Andreas Müller: I would almost say that's exactly how it is.

Justin Allen: I'm just repeating what I said. And then you came and said that's actually exactly how it is. And then we said, just by the definition of the me being born, means that it's there.

Andreas Müller: Yeah.

Justin Allen: And that's what you're saying is, starting off like this and then trying to get back into the loaf of bread.

Andreas Müller: In the personal experience, the experience is "I'm there." The person doesn't experience the process of separation from the whole. All it knows is, "I'm separate." Because self-awareness is this notion, this seeming knowing, "I'm separate," this recognition of "I am. I'm separate." And in a way, (laughs) to live and to die, or to meet this message and to die, to be killed, is being forced back into wholeness. It's not a path that the me would take because, of course, as we talked about, the me doesn't really want to die into wholeness.

Justin Allen: Because it loses itself.

Andreas Müller: Because it loses itself. It wants to be there and experience something that it would hope that this would be wholeness.

Justin Allen: I can't help but think of this biologically, that you start off in a woman's stomach.

Andreas Müller: Without any kind of self-awareness, and even live outside that womb without self-awareness.

Justin Allen: The mom, in a way, is like the loaf of bread. (laughs) And then you exit (detach from) it, and then for a while you're still kind of like the loaf of bread. But then at some point, you're there, then.

Andreas Müller: Yeah.

Justin Allen: You don't necessarily want to go back to mom anymore, and you can't. So then you're forced to search, or it's really like you're forced to search in life, whether it's spiritual or otherwise.

Andreas Müller: Absolutely.

Justin Allen: You're fucked, having to be searching.

Andreas Müller: Until you are pulled back. Not because you want it. The me doesn't want those meetings or this message. The seeker would love if the seeking would pay off, if its methods pay off. It doesn't want to die. It would have much more preferred if the guru was right.

Justin Allen: You know when you're in a relationship with somebody, and then you break up, and then you get back together? And it feels very good when you get back together, even if you think, "Oh, I shouldn't be with this person?" But every time that you disconnect and then connect again, it's like you're reliving this good feeling.

Andreas Müller: Yeah, but this wouldn't have anything to do with liberation.

Justin Allen: It has to do with that searching thing and feeling like...because that's a sense where you've unioned, you've gone back to the whole because you and your girlfriend or you and your wife were the whole that you created in your life that you could also experience. And that's why those things like getting my first million is a great experience because I feel like, "Wow, I've fulfilled everything."

Andreas Müller: Yeah, "I gained something from having that million."

Justin Allen: Yeah. But I feel fulfilled. I feel a wholeness when I've done that, and I feel a wholeness when I've found my partner that's perfect for me.

Andreas Müller:	"When I have an insight. When this and this happens, and this and this." Yeah, yeah, of course.
Justin Allen:	And then when you lose a million, then you're lost. Desperate. You're fighting to get it back, or else you've picked something else to go get. With the relationship thing, when you break up, and then come back together, and break up, and come back together, and some people might do that, the whole relationship when they're together for 50 years.
Andreas Müller:	Or just break up and come together with someone new and break up and come together with someone new and...
Justin Allen:	I'm trying to use the one where you're in one relationship with one person. You separate, and that feeling is good because you get to experience it, because you're there feeling like you were lost, and now you're whole again.
Andreas Müller:	Yes, but I think it's this assumption that there is something deeper in that. It's not the gaining of a million; it's the assumption that having a million is already a pre-expectation, the me sets up the value thinking owning a million is worthwhile as if it has a deeper value to earn a million. So in this moment, when you have that million, this assumption, "Great. I achieved something. This gave me something on a deeper level." And the same, this lovely feeling when you become a partner again, there's this, "Ahh (sigh of relief), now I gained something again." And, of course, the other way around, when this splits up, or when you lose the money, it really feels as if, "Oh dear, I lose my fulfillment." But it's always connected to this impression of a deeper value it has. It's never the thing itself.
Justin Allen:	Probably, a psychologist... That's the pattern that you're going to see in every human being, in a way.

Losing and trying to gain something. Losing and trying to gain something.

Andreas Müller: To me, it's not a psychological problem. To me, it's really...

Justin Allen: They would see it as a psychological...

Andreas Müller: They would see it...exactly.

Justin Allen: That's what I mean. We would see it that way, also. Because we've been trained to also think...

Andreas Müller: Spiritual people would see it as a spiritual problem. Therapists would see it as a psychological problem. Everyone would see it as a problem in their context.

Justin Allen: Psychiatry, at least in Germany and America. It's seeped into everything. Spirituality isn't into everything. But my friend that I grew up with is a hand worker, and he was educated worse than I was...

Andreas Müller: Sorry, but 300 years ago, religion was into everything. Religion was spirituality 300 years ago, and it was in all parts of society.

Justin Allen: But now psychology has permeated everything. The average person, no matter what, if they run into a problem with their wife, or at work, or with their boss, they're going to say, "Man, I need to work on myself, or I need to."

Andreas Müller: Exactly. (laughs) So, it's just replaced it.

Justin Allen: Yeah.

Andreas Müller: The modern spirituality, so to speak, is psychology in that sense.

Justin Allen: That is the pattern that all seekers are stuck in, in a way. Even that duality is necessary, to get, and then lose it. And get it again, and lose it...

Andreas Müller: Well, it's not necessary. It just is the person's experience. Duality.

Justin Allen: I also think you need it because you want the feeling...

Andreas Müller: Yeah, of course.

Justin Allen: I'm using the pattern of... certain people are in a relationship with each other where they're constantly breaking up and getting back together and breaking up. It's because they crave it. That's where they get their high, and their excitement is that great feeling when they join again.

Andreas Müller: Yeah. Oh, that's why the person loves the world and loves existence because it's dependent on it. Of course. It needs a playground. It needs a possibility to have an experience of fulfillment. And that's only possible in a real dual world. With a picture of the bread and the bread crumb, I don't say that, originally, there is something like wholeness in terms of this whole bread. It's only the separate part that creates the image of there being bread, also. And that's the basic duality. Wholeness and me, as if there were two real things, and as if we can meet again as an experience. That's me and my partner, that's me and the million, that's me and the world. But as I say, the person is dependent on there being this other reality because that's where its fulfillment will take place.

Justin Allen: But still, your description of this is that all there is, is wholeness. That is it.

Andreas Müller: Yeah, but it's not a circumstance.

Justin Allen:

It's still, "This is wholeness," and part of this wholeness is still the illusion of separation.

Andreas Müller:

Which is also wholeness. This separation never actually happened. That's what this message is saying: that it's an illusion and not something real.

Justin Allen:

Right now, where you said the loaf of bread, and then there's a crumb that gets removed, and it's in another location, let's say. In your description of wholeness, that crumb is never removed from the whole loaf of bread. But somehow, within that, there's a fake individual.

Andreas Müller:

Yeah, if you want so.

Justin Allen:

You could also try to describe it using the loaf of bread saying that there's a crumb that somehow... even though it's still not away from the loaf, that it somehow shrinks.

Even that is a better way. Let's say that, that crumb that's 5mm by 5mm by 5mm, all of a sudden, within that loaf, it constricts, which means it decreases. So it goes from 5 by 5 by 5...

Andreas Müller:

...to something more dense or tight, yeah. (laughs)

Justin Allen:

It's still part of the loaf. It hasn't been removed from the loaf. But, somehow because of that contraction, it creates a false sense that it's separated.

Andreas Müller:

Yes. Kind of.

Justin Allen:

You can't describe it any better than that. (laughs)

Andreas Müller:

(laughs) I can't describe it at all. Exactly. Because we are already operating in this, "There is a thing called wholeness, and there is something that becomes apart." That's not what I'm saying, that wholeness is like...

Justin Allen:	No, but you do say that all there is, is wholeness.
Andreas Müller:	Yeah, but what I actually mean is all there is, is what seems to be happening. And that's whole and complete.
Justin Allen:	You could still say that exact sentence and equate that to being a loaf of bread.
Andreas Müller:	Yes and no, because then it would be something else.
Justin Allen:	But all there is, is loaf of bread. That's it. There's only loaf of bread.
Andreas Müller:	Yeah, without a beginning and an end. Without being something.
Justin Allen:	Exactly. For us, in a diagrammatic world, right now we're sitting in blackness. There's nothing. Blackness isn't anything. There's nothing in the blackness. But then there's a loaf of bread. And within that loaf of bread, there's some little 5 by 5 by 5 (mm) area that contracts. And because of that contraction, it creates an illusion of separation from that wholeness.
Andreas Müller:	Exactly, but what's actually being said here is that there isn't even a contraction; not even in the loaf of bread.
Justin Allen:	But that would be the best way to talk about this contraction, also. Because that was one of my other questions; this contraction doesn't happen either.
Andreas Müller:	Exactly.
Justin Allen:	This sense of self doesn't actually happen.
Andreas Müller:	Exactly, or the illusion of that is what seems to be happening. But you can't go there really, as much

as you can't say if this table is happening or the floor is happening, or if this is happening. Because then you already operate in an objectified reality. And that's just not what this is. It just isn't an objectified reality. Not even one big object, the loaf of bread, that's made out of many small objects. That's just not what this...

Justin Allen:

...is. Right, but the loaf of bread wouldn't be an object either in the way that I'm talking about it.

Andreas Müller:

There would be just bread. Yeah, exactly. The surprise is that this would be the bread.

Justin Allen:

Yeah. This would be the bread here, too.

Andreas Müller:

Exactly. It's not that actually, all of this is something else; namely wholeness or the loaf of bread. This is the bread. We were talking about how separation never actually happened. That's how we started this morning, that this claim to be someone is also just what's happening or what apparently happens. It's never real, in that sense.

Justin Allen:

I was thinking about contraction because I asked you in the first half of the meeting, what you guys mean by "contraction." And we also said that contraction doesn't actually happen. But you described it in a way that...physically you pulled your arm into your chest and you got tightened up and you made yourself compact and smaller by tightening.

Andreas Müller:

Yeah.

Justin Allen:

And then you said "the me," the person, the seeker, can relate to that because that's how they feel when their full neuroses come up.

Andreas Müller:

Exactly. I sometimes call it a subtle sense of presence. That's a bit more neutral. But I think most people just feel tense and contracted as if they have to pay attention. As if they have to be there and consciously do life. I think that's what's meant with this energy. It just feels, "I'm here. I'm now here. I'm something. I've become real. I've become concrete, and I have to do life." I think that's where this picture of a contracted energy comes from.

Justin Allen: If the contracted energy was to die and not be there anymore, then it should be the opposite of contraction.

Andreas Müller: Yes, but of course what the person understands is an opposite experience; an experience of freedom and boundlessness.

Justin Allen: Yeah, but only using words. If we accept that there's contraction, then the opposite of that would either be expansion or relaxation.

Andreas Müller: Yeah, I would call that boundlessness.

Justin Allen: Boundlessness is also a little bit like expansion (which) could expand infinitely. But it's also just a sense of being more open and free. If you think of contraction, then, in the way that you're talking about it, expansion seems a little bit like you're expanding and getting bigger. Relaxation also works in a way that if you're not there anymore, you're not tightening up.

Andreas Müller: And there isn't the stress of seeking anymore.

Justin Allen: I think relaxation might be a better opposite word of contraction in this context. It's the vernacular of our day and age right now. You hear something like, "Just let go." Everybody's tenser now than they used to be because we have social media and we have so many options available to us. And we're all too tight, and we just need to "relax and let go."

And there's a feeling like you can't relax and let go because if you do, you're giving up control. And who's going to do that, and how is that going to get done? So, relaxation almost has a negative context for us in the sense that it's almost like we're not going to be here anymore if we relax. If we relax too much, we will just vanish.

Andreas Müller: Yeah. Can't stop doing it. Need to stay present. Also, in spirituality, of course. (laughs)

Justin Allen: Yeah.

Andreas Müller: Too much letting go isn't experienced as good. There's the danger of losing track. So that's why there's a big emphasis on being present and not losing the path and stuff like that. One can become so relaxed that one could lose oneself. That's why there's always a little bit of effort in even being aware. It already needs some effort. It's not relaxed.

Justin Allen: So, relaxation or something fully relaxed is con- ceptually not there. If you really totally let go and relaxed, the sense or the feeling that I have is that I wouldn't be here anymore. There'd be nothing here.

Andreas Müller: Exactly. Yeah. Which is, in a very funny way, what this message points out; that everything is totally re- laxed. Everything just is itself mainly because there is no one.

Justin Allen: Even the person that appears to be very tense and stressed out and tight.

Andreas Müller: In the end, that too. Yeah.

Justin Allen: I don't know if this makes sense, I'll just read what I have, but I wrote, "Nothing somehow contracts (laughs) and this contraction appears to happen, although it doesn't really happen. And then the contraction essentially seeks to un-contract itself."

Andreas Müller: Yeah, but only up to a certain point. That's what we talked about. Only as much as it still can enjoy its own relaxation. It doesn't want to relax into death, so to speak.

Justin Allen: I wrote also that the contraction, which isn't really contracting or happening, is also the dissatisfaction and the seeking.

Andreas Müller: Yeah, exactly. It's an illusion. This whole personal world is an illusion. That's not logical. That can't be explained or understood or... all the person can do is to believe in that, but that's futile.

Justin Allen: You said that you went through a two-year period where you were fading away. Let's say that you were six months away from the completely fading away point. Did you have thoughts when you were trying to contemplate whatever deep things you might have been trying to contemplate at the time that you couldn't contemplate them? Let's say four years ago, before you died or five years ago, you could contemplate a bunch of philosophical ideas. And you might say, "What is (a) me? Am I really here or not?" And then as you started to fade away, you just lost all interest in any kind of contemplations?

Andreas Müller: One could say so, yeah; at least lost more and more interest in it.

Justin Allen: And it instead was taken over a little bit, like, "I'm not sure I'm here."

Andreas Müller: One could say so, yeah. It wasn't really that this was taking up, but yeah. It's automatic, the less interest you have in those things. It's not only that the interest faded out, but this whole energy was just less and less there, or less and less in the foreground. But in the story, it would have looked like, "Yeah, I don't care that much anymore," or, "Who knows," or " Hmm, I really can't say if I'm "a me" or not." So this would still be going on, but there would be much more uncertainty about things. There was much more uncertainty about all those things and questions, but surprisingly it didn't matter that much.

Justin Allen: That's what I mean. Whatever uncertainty or doubt or questioning came up...The old you and the conditioning of you or the familiarity of you, you could be like, "Normally, I would want to try to get a hold of this and understand it. And now, even if I wanted to, I couldn't."

Andreas Müller: I couldn't and, the surprise, that it didn't matter even; that I didn't need to know this; that life just went on without me understanding or knowing it. And there was already a confidence in that. I mean, there was still the attempt and, still, the idea that I could know, or that there is something to know or to become. But, the not happening of that didn't matter. Life just went on and it was fine.

Justin Allen: We're doing a pretty big leap right now when we go into this. (laughs) I'm asking it out of curiosity because it happened. You give talks for ten years, let's say. And at some point, you had zero people interested, and it grew. And then, let's say five years ago, you got a certain number, and it stayed that same with maybe a slight increase.

Andreas Müller: Yeah.

Justin Allen: It's similar to the other guys that are as known as you are in this topic. Jim Newman and Kenneth Madden are the ones I'm most familiar with. And then Tony Parsons is a little bit ahead of everybody, but he started 30 or 40 years ago and he's kind of the godfather in the sense that even though there might have been other people with the same message, he's the one that brought it out to the general public (relatively recently), and the general public replied with positivity.

Andreas Müller: Yeah.

Justin Allen: We also see that there are new people that come into this. I've been paying attention to this for four years, roughly. I've seen a group of 20-year-olds that came into the scene sounding very similar to you. I've also seen a couple of other people around your age that have come in and also sounded similar, and then they disappeared for whatever reason, or I didn't gravitate towards them. But Neil Denham is an example of somebody that I thought sounded nice. But he was only there maybe for a year? And then, a little bit older than you but not that much older, is Rupert Spira and Mooji. And then you have Adyashanti and then Eckhart Tolle. And Eckhart Tolle is the king of somehow claiming the idea of not being there, but in a different way, of there being oneness or consciousness. The spiritual ones. You're related in some way to the spiritual people, whether you like it or not. From the general public, you're just categorized in that group.

Andreas Müller: Absolutely, yeah.

Justin Allen: And even if you post a book, your book's going to be sold in the same category.

Andreas Müller: Yeah, yeah.

Justin Allen:	You're part of that world. You can't separate your-self from it, from the perspective of the audience.
Andreas Müller:	Absolutely, yeah.
Justin Allen:	If you compare the amount of numbers that you have to Rupert Spira; if you're both trying to earn your income from giving talks and books, his should be much higher than yours. (laughs)
Andreas Müller:	(laughs) I guess that's how it is.
Justin Allen:	Mooji also, and Adyashanti also, and then Eckhart Tolle is another way higher level above Rupert Spi-ra and Adyashanti. In this world of people that are interested in this, they're aware that there's ... not a conflict, but if I go to a Kenneth Madden talk, or a Jim Newman talk, somebody might bring up Rupert Spira or Eckhart Tolle. And also, if I go to a Rupert Spira or an Adyashanti or Eckhart Tolle, people do bring up at least Tony Parsons. I've seen that myself firsthand. You would claim that there are similarities, but at the most fundamental level, then it's almost a radical difference.
Andreas Müller:	Yes, some words might sound similar. I don't think there are more similarities than that some words sound similar. I don't see other similarities because, energetically, it's something completely different.
Justin Allen:	From the perspective of an audience, they could see a lot of similarities.
Andreas Müller:	Yes. I can follow that. I can acknowledge, so to speak, that at a superficial look, it can seem like the same.
Justin Allen:	The people who would be interested in your mes-sage, you're not capturing them from Eckhart Tolle, but you're capturing them from the spiritual world. If we say the only types of people in the world are

spiritual seekers, love seekers, monetary seekers, or power seekers; if there are only those four categories...

Andreas Müller: Yeah, and we put the psychology in the spiritual.

Justin Allen: You're capturing more of the psychology, and spiritual ones than you are of the monetary and romance ones.

Andreas Müller: Yeah.

Justin Allen: And same with them. The spiritual teachers like Adyashanti and Eckhart Tolle are also capturing people that are (mostly) just spiritual seekers more so than they're capturing monetary seekers.

Andreas Müller: It's mixing up, exactly. Because a lot of money seekers think that they can use spirituality to make more money.

Justin Allen: Or for whatever reason. His message is going to cross their radar because Eckhart Tolle was on Oprah Winfrey, for example. If you ended up on some kind of big broadcast, then you might also attract monetary and romance and those kinds of seekers.

Andreas Müller: Yeah, maybe.

Justin Allen: But that hasn't happened. (both laugh) The only reason I'm bringing this up is because sometimes, I try to think of how other people might think of this message. And, to get to my point, nobody in your category earns a lot of money doing this, comparatively.

Andreas Müller: Yep.

Justin Allen: And, if we just name Adyashanti, Rupert Spira, Mooji, and Eckhart Tolle, they earn a lot of money.

Andreas Müller:	They're almost companies. It's not just one person saying something.
Justin Allen:	And you've written ten books? And I think Eckhart Tolle. maybe has written two. (both laugh)
Andreas Müller:	But the thing is, in my ten books, it's always the same, isn't it? (laughs) No, it's very different. That's the funny thing about it. The first book is, "All There Is Is This Moment," and the second book is, "A New Earth." That's where he told everyone how we can create a new earth, which is a total contradiction of his first book where all that exists is this moment.
Justin Allen:	I couldn't help but have this thought. From you giving these talks and from Kenneth Madden giving these talks and all these, let's say, five people that are similar to you, why wouldn't any of you just give the same message as Adyashanti?
Andreas Müller:	Oh, because it's an impossibility when the person collapses.
Justin Allen:	So if you couldn't earn money doing this, what you're doing right now unless you want to be homeless or not have the things that you currently have, you'd have to get a job.
Andreas Müller:	Yeah, of course.
Justin Allen:	And then at the age of mid-40s, what jobs you can get, you'd be somewhat more limited than you could have been when you were in your 20s.
Andreas Müller:	Oh yeah, of course.
Justin Allen:	What you can get around here (job-wise, in this town), you'd try to find something because you also have family and you can't just relocate unless you want to abandon your family.

Andreas Müller:	Exactly, I would just look for a job here. It would be alright.
Justin Allen:	So you'd just find some kind of mediocre local job and it would pay you enough to have your rent and live at the standard that you're currently living in.
Andreas Müller:	That's the hope, yeah. (both laugh) Something like this.
Justin Allen:	The plan B. So why would that be worse? Let's say the only job opening is that you have to work in the hair salon, and you don't even know how to cut hair. So you have to wash people's scalps, and then you learn the trade a bit, and after a year or two, you're cutting hair. Why is that better than just giving the message of Adyashanti where you might have the potential to earn a lot of money?
Andreas Müller:	Oh, because there just isn't anyone.
Justin Allen:	Yeah, but why does it matter?
Andreas Müller:	Well, I don't say that it matters. I would just say it's an impossibility. Not because it matters. But because there is no one.
Justin Allen:	No one where?
Andreas Müller:	Here.
Justin Allen:	Yeah, but you're still saying that it's impossible for you, for the "no one" there, to work in the field of Adyashanti, but it's not impossible for you to work at Edeka (a food-market chain in Germany).
Andreas Müller:	Yeah, because it's totally based on this illusion that there is someone. Being a spiritual teacher is based on the impression that there is an awareness that can teach awareness and which can help awareness.

Justin Allen:	But I still don't see why you'd be limited to conveying that message.
Andreas Müller:	Because it's conveying limitation.
Justin Allen:	Being a hair cutter also has limitations, and the people that come in there think that they're "there" also.
Andreas Müller:	The people who come to the talks also think that I'm someone.
Justin Allen:	But they think that you're cutting their hair.
Andreas Müller:	Yeah, but that's all right.
Justin Allen:	But why isn't it alright also to, kind of give a spiritual message, to people that think that they're there... why is that service so dissimilar than...
Andreas Müller:	Oh, because it is impossible.
Justin Allen:	What?
Andreas Müller:	Because it's impossible.
Justin Allen:	You're saying that you are restricted to giving the service of telling people that they're there, but you're not restricted to giving the service of cutting somebody's hair?
Andreas Müller:	Well, I think you can't put it like that.
Justin Allen:	Why not?
Andreas Müller:	Because it's not a restriction.
Justin Allen:	What isn't a restriction?
Andreas Müller:	It's not a restriction to not be able to teach people, or to be "a me."

Justin Allen:	That's essentially the one job that you're saying you can't do. Every other job would be available to you.
Andreas Müller:	Well, no. I couldn't be a priest, a psychiatrist, a philosopher; all those things which only speak to "the me."
Justin Allen:	What about a school teacher?
Andreas Müller:	Difficult. (laughs) But I would be able to because you can be a teacher or a parent without the assumption that you need to educate a small "me."
Justin Allen:	What about somebody who takes care of old people?
Andreas Müller:	Yeah, of course. Why not?
Justin Allen:	I don't know.
Andreas Müller:	And the same with the hairdresser. I mean, people think that there is a "me" who has a body, and whose hair gets cut, but it's basically just what seems to be happening.
Justin Allen:	But the reason why you couldn't be a priest, a spiritual teacher, a psychologist, or psychiatrist is...you can't answer the question, you're just saying that you couldn't do it.
Andreas Müller:	Because there is "no one." I don't see how this is...
Justin Allen:	... how it's possible for you to do that job.
Andreas Müller:	Absolutely.
Justin Allen:	But don't you think a lot of times that jobs are doing things that you can't (don't want to) do, and you (laughs) do them anyways to earn money?

Andreas Müller: No.

Justin Allen: You don't think that?

Andreas Müller: All of that just is what seems to be happening.

Justin Allen: Yeah, but then what would seem to be happening is, if you have to earn money, you have to work at Edeka. If you go around this neighborhood and the openings are priest, Edeka or hair salon, you're not going to...

Andreas Müller: Well, I could become a non-dual speaker disguised as a priest. Why not? Standing in front of a cross, I would tell them that there is no God; if they still think that I'm a priest (laughs) with a weird expression of Christianity? Oh, that would be possible.

Justin Allen: Why would it be so impossible for you to lie, basically? What's so hard about that?

Andreas Müller: Because there is "no one."

Justin Allen: Yeah, but why would it be so difficult to say (laughs) that there is "someone?"

Andreas Müller: Because there is "no one."

Justin Allen: I don't understand why it would be so difficult to lie about it.

Andreas Müller: Oh, because there isn't even someone there who could lie about it.

Justin Allen: You would also say there is "no one" there that can not lie about it; that can tell what they think the truth is.

Andreas Müller: There just is "no one." Exactly.

Justin Allen:	Yeah, but there is "no one" that's willing to cut hair, but this one that isn't there, isn't willing to priest or spiritual teach.
Andreas Müller:	Yep.
Justin Allen:	That's...
Andreas Müller:	... not logical.
Justin Allen:	I don't know if it's not logical, but what if the only job here was to be a priest?
Andreas Müller:	I would starve, then.
Justin Allen:	(laughs) You'd choose starving over having food? (laughs)
Andreas Müller:	As I said, I would be a non-dual priest.
Justin Allen:	Well, that was a curious question for me, because...
Andreas Müller:	Oh, it's an impossibility.
Justin Allen:	You think it's an impossibility?
Andreas Müller:	Absolutely. It only comes off being someone, and the illusion to be someone. Only. There is no other thing that's about. It only comes from this illusion and serves this illusion.
Justin Allen:	To put it in the context of everyday life or common life, a hand worker might say, "I could never have a desk job."
Andreas Müller:	Yeah, but that's something else.
Justin Allen:	What if it's a hand worker that isn't there?
Andreas Müller:	(both laugh) Then it's something else. I mean, that's in the story.

Justin Allen:	What's in the story? How is that different than anything we've been talking about that's not in the story?
Andreas Müller:	Well, that was also in the story. But, of course, with the handyman, it would be a personal preference. He would say, "I could never do a desk job because it's not fun," or something.
Justin Allen:	I think that there are people that, without an explanation, can't do certain jobs. They refuse to. But you're saying something different.
Andreas Müller:	Exactly. It's something completely different. It's a bit like, as if you ask, "Can seeking still happen when there is no me?" No, of course not, because "the me" is seeking. And it's not a limitation that seeking can't happen anymore. That's actually what you're asking because teaching is seeking. It's just the same, coming from the same experience and coming from the same narrative. So, that's what you're asking, actually.
Justin Allen:	So it's like... (laughs) it's like you're kryptonite. It's something that you just can't do, no matter what. You can't be a spiritual teacher or anything similar.
Andreas Müller:	Yeah, prefer the cross.
Justin Allen:	But you could, for example, be a football coach.
Andreas Müller:	Probably, yeah.
Justin Allen:	Because that's okay, in the sense that you're just teaching somebody how to kick a football and pass.
Andreas Müller:	It's bodies. Yeah.
Justin Allen:	And doing something like investing in a stock market, that wouldn't be objectionable.

Andreas Müller:	Oh, that could happen. If there would be enough income...
Justin Allen:	If you had money to invest with. (both laugh)
Andreas Müller:	Yeah, why not?
Justin Allen:	Let's say that Eckhart Tolle becomes successful as an interviewer.
Andreas Müller:	(laughs) He turns into Oprah.
Justin Allen:	Do you know Oprah Winfrey?
Andreas Müller:	Not really.
Justin Allen:	I don't know if she still has her show or not, but if she does and Eckhart Tolle replaced her and started to have his own people on for interviewing, would you agree to be interviewed by him?
Andreas Müller:	I'm not sure, actually.
Justin Allen:	Because you feel like, it (the message) might get manipulated?
Andreas Müller:	Well, it depends. If the interest is about what I say, then yes. But if it's for his own purposes, for his show or...It's not even that they want to invite me as the person, Andreas Müller. The moment they want to invite the message and are open and curious about this message, I go, whoever it is. But the moment that's not given, I think there wouldn't be a resonance to go.
Justin Allen:	If this message ever got the same kind of excitement and population behind it as the spiritual message gets, that would be exciting, no?
Andreas Müller:	No. It would just be what happens. I don't know if it would be more exciting than it already is. (laughs)

Justin Allen:	Do you notice any kind of change? If you have a larger audience, is there some kind of change in the atmosphere?
Andreas Müller:	Yeah, of course. In one way, it's different if there are five people or 25 people, but in another way, it's not different at all.
Justin Allen:	Do you ever have children in your audience?
Andreas Müller:	Hardly, very hardly (rarely).
Justin Allen:	Would you object to the children in the audience?
Andreas Müller:	No. They are just mostly busy becoming a "me" and still enjoying having it all ahead of them. (both laugh) I have some people who say they were actually seeking when they were four or five, desperately seeking the meaning of life. So, if a kid would end up in the meeting and asking about the meaning of life, there would just be a clear answer. But most kids just don't seek, in that sense.
Justin Allen:	And do you ever listen to anybody for longer periods, just out of interest to see how they talk about it differently?
Andreas Müller:	No.
Justin Allen:	So, more or less, Tony Parsons was the last person you heard other than yourself talk about this.
Andreas Müller:	The only person, and the last person.
Justin Allen:	What about your parents or your brother? Have they ever expressed interest in your message?
Andreas Müller:	No. My mother did, somehow. But not the others.
Justin Allen:	Do you ever have a wish to share it with them?

Andreas Müller: No.

Justin Allen: And how far did it go with your mother?

Andreas Müller: Well, it did go that far as she was...

Justin Allen: ...as she wanted to. Where did it end for her? (both laugh) When you said, "You're not there, mom?"

Andreas Müller: (laughs) Well, yeah.

Justin Allen: That's where it ended for her? Did she come to a meeting?

Andreas Müller: When I started, yeah. And just recently, she's been there for a few minutes.

Justin Allen: And when you go to a family...Christmas or Easter would be the big family thing? There might be ten people related to you there. Do you feel like they treat you a little bit dis-similar than if you had, let's say, a job at Edeka or?

Andreas Müller: (laughs) They are treating me better now. (laughs) No, just normal.

Justin Allen: Just to put it in a conventional term, if somebody goes to their family, do you sit down and somebody says, "So, how's the job?"

Andreas Müller: Yeah, exactly, that can happen.

Justin Allen: And then what do you say?

Andreas Müller: Good.

Justin Allen: That's it?

Andreas Müller: Yeah.

Justin Allen:

Do they ever make jokes? You know, when you have your talks, people make jokes like, "Oh, I'm not here. Ha ha ha."

Andreas Müller:

Not at all. They don't go there at all. They don't go to the message at all. I'm sure most of them haven't ever read one word.

Justin Allen:

Do you feel like, consciously, they're actively avoiding asking you because they don't want to hear any sermons?

Andreas Müller:

No, it's even more pushed away. It's already pushed away. They don't even come to consciously push it away. It doesn't happen. It's not an issue.

COULD YOU BE A SPIRITUAL TEACHER?

Justin Allen:	What I wanted to do today, just because from our talk yesterday, towards the end of our conversation, when I asked you about teachers, and if you could be a teacher. You answered it, but I felt like I wasn't confident with my understanding or what you were trying to communicate. And then after we stopped recording, we continued with the conversation and I felt, then, that I understood better what your answer was. It felt more like your original answer made sense to me, whereas it didn't before.
Andreas Müller:	All right.
Justin Allen:	If I try to paraphrase it, I asked, could you become a teacher? Teacher meaning a spiritual teacher teacher. And the way that I prefaced it all, was by pointing out that the way that you communicate this message, it seems very unlikely that you will be monetarily successful. And, comparatively, these spiritual teachers seem to be successful financially with their teaching. So then I thought about how, in the end, sometimes you just have to have a job. You just need to earn money.
Andreas Müller:	Yep.
Justin Allen:	And then you would choose which job is possible for me (you), where I (you) could earn a substantial amount of money. In a simple sense, it's not such

a leap to go from what you've been doing for ten years to spiritual teaching.

Andreas Müller: Being a spiritual teacher, yeah. (laughs)

Justin Allen: It was prefaced under those circumstances, and you said, "I can't do it," basically. And I said, "Why?" And then you say, "Because there's no me." And I didn't understand how (what) you're saying. Because there's "no me" (no one) in the audience? Or does it mean that there's "no me" there where you are? It wasn't a satisfactory answer for me.

Andreas Müller: Yeah. That's what I meant when I was answering yesterday that there is "no one" here. I know when I say there is "no one" in a general sense, it sounds so much like knowledge or dogma. "I can't do that. I'm not allowed. I'm not supposed to do it because I know that actually there is no one. So it would be bad" or something. No, how I meant it is much, much more direct. We are operating in the story here anyway, and in the story (there) are no true answers, if you want. So it's all stories anyway. But in the story, I would have to say, there's just really no one here with me. This apparent illusion really has collapsed, and that's why it would just be impossible. It's not just impossible out of a choice. I'm not even there to choose A or B. It's not that it would be a conscious choice. "Oh, I can't do that because there is no one here." It can't happen. What I just said yesterday, I think, was right to the point, actually. It is as if you asked me, "Could you still seek?" That's an impossibility when the person collapses because the person is the seeker or the teacher.

Justin Allen: I think that answer, is more to the point as someone hearing this message. For me to qualify what you said, it's because when there's "no me," then you can't teach...

Andreas Müller: ...another "me."

Justin Allen: Exactly. You can't teach to promote this idea of "a me." But also, you can't teach in the sense of spiritual teaching when there's no one there. By definition, to be a spiritual teacher or to be some kind of teacher who is confirming "a me" to somebody else requires there to be "a me." So it's the same as we said yesterday: you can't teach mathematics to somebody unless you are an expert in mathematics. Generally, that's what we say is to teach, you have to be an expert in something.

Andreas Müller: Yeah, you have to at least know more than the other one.

Justin Allen: So, by default, to be a spiritual teacher means that you have kind of mastered... you've got a Ph. D. in being someone.

Andreas Müller: ...in being "a me." That's what they all are.

Justin Allen: In that sense, it's very simple to say if there's "no me," then I'm no longer an expert in this category. And I'm not able to teach it because it doesn't exist for me. This whole "The me isn't there and there are no me's listening to the message. So there's nothing there...."

Andreas Müller: Yeah, kind of. In my story one could almost say I have been an expert in that because most of my life being someone, I was a spiritual seeker. So, I theoretically could do it. But I just died.

Justin Allen: If I was a mathematics professor, and then we discovered that math is not real. It's a totally fake thing. This whole idea of math that seemed like it was the right thing. It seemed like you could add numbers, and then they would equal something, and we could use it to prove things and develop formulas. But in the end, somehow, we figured out no, math was just fake.

Andreas Müller:

Yeah, I get the picture. And the picture is right on the one hand. On the other hand, it is still a personal picture with a choice. Because in this picture, theoretically, you could still be lying. You could still choose to lie and teach mathematics knowingly that it's not what you thought it to be. But when the personal energy collapses, it's just not there anymore. So, it's not a choice in that sense. But the other part of the picture is right, one could say.

Justin Allen:

So that's kind of resolved. (both laugh)

Andreas Müller:

But the question was a bit, "But why can you do this, and not this?" But when the personal energy collapses, it, of course, collapses completely. It's not just that, in the spiritual world, there is no person anymore. So even when I would do another job or another job would happen, I still wouldn't address the customers or the clients as if they were "me's." Of course, my appearance, so to speak, would look like, as in a meeting, that this is just talking ordinarily. What else? And this would, of course, happen there as well. But also clients, people, colleagues, the boss, whoever wouldn't be addressed as being someone because this energy just isn't there anymore.

Justin Allen:

But (for) a lot of those jobs, that's okay. Nobody would register that it doesn't matter. But with a specific job like being a spiritual teacher or a job that needs you to confirm "me's..."

Andreas Müller:

That's what the whole thing is about. That only happens because there is this illusion of "me," apparently. That's the interesting thing with this message, that's where this concept just doesn't work. If you have this concept, "All just is what seems to be happening," because then you would need to ask, "Why is this not possible? If everything just is what seems to be happening, and everything is possible, why can't this happen? And why can't this happen?" And that shows that this sentence, "That's just what seems to be happening," is not a concept at all. It's not a general truth, in a sense, how the person would understand it, which is an explanation to everything and which kind of seems to make everything possible. Even things that seem illogical or something. So, in that sense, this message is way more incomprehensible and not dogmatic at all, and not presenting any concepts or truths, in a sense, how the person would see it. Because there would always be the question, "Yeah, but why couldn't it just be what seems to be happening?" Like, "Andreas Müller, could you become a seeker again?" or "Can there be seeking without a me?"

Justin Allen: Which I asked in our first…

Andreas Müller: We talked about, yeah. For example, "Can there be seeking without a me?" And I say, "Well no. Of course not, because the me is seeking. And the me would ask back, 'yeah, but if it is what seems to be happening, eeeeeeee! No!'" (laughs)

Justin Allen: But with the teacher one, I think that's a theme that I was aware of in your talks and other talks similar; that, that comes up a lot. And you and everybody else with this message very often get addressed as being a teacher or almost like a guru. And then sometimes, if you're diligent enough, you correct them. And sometimes you don't. So it's just automatically a consequence of this message somehow being seemingly related to spirituality, that it has to almost be addressed in every meeting in some way. You guys, you have to come out and say, in your opening five-minute speech, "I'm not a teacher. This isn't a teaching." But it's not that effective. It doesn't break through the audience, necessarily.

Andreas Müller:	No.
Justin Allen:	I was trying to find another way to address this; to take the premise why you couldn't ever be a teacher. Another thing that we could talk about is, we talked about it in the talk about how you kind of live an ordinary life, and this message is ultimately ordinary, and your message is also relatively ordinary, or the atmosphere around it is; without bells and whistles, (without) meaning. That's what I mean by ordinary. There's not something, extreme or shocking or...
Andreas Müller:	...Or artificial. It's not artificially made shiny.
Justin Allen:	For you, that's also not a contrivance. It's not something that you strive for. It's just naturally that way.
Andreas Müller:	Yes, exactly. So everything is naturally itself. The natural reality is natural. Harmony is natural. Again, it's not an artificial naturalness. With some Buddhists, for example. I have the impression that there is sometimes an artificial naturalness as if they play natural or childlike, or... that's how it feels to me, at least. And this has nothing to do with that. Everything just is naturally what it is.
Justin Allen:	You mean like kissing children's tongues? (both laugh)
Andreas Müller:	As far as I've heard, that's a very old tradition, so it's all fine. (both laugh) I guess there was an innocent smile involved in that, too, I don't know if it was before or afterward. But it's both things. In a way, this is ordinary, which the person would relate to, "Okay, it's my normal life or my day-to-day experience." And on the other hand, what's also pointed out is that this total harmony, and not being someone, and to not live in this personal world, is also totally ordinary. But it is total harmony. It's not ordinary in

the sense that the person would understand the ordinary, which is always boring, and what it wants to escape from. People don't like each other. There's always a struggle. There's always something to do. I'm responsible for my fulfillment. I'm responsible for money. I'm me me me. That's what the person would regard as ordinary. But part of this is what we talked about yesterday, this looking for this special thing. No. Not being someone is ordinary, and this perfect harmony is ordinary. But it's also perfect harmony.

Justin Allen: Just to create another scenario, there are also "me's" that are living what we might consider extraordinary lives, like a very wealthy entrepreneur or a famous actor.

Andreas Müller: Or a spiritual teacher. (laughs)

Justin Allen: And then there are ordinary people that live ordinary lives. And there are "me's" still living an ordinary, under-the-radar type of life.

Andreas Müller: I think 99 percent of all people are like that, probably.

Justin Allen: But, on paper, your life is as ordinary as these other 99...

Andreas Müller: Oh yeah, of course. In the end, every life is ordinary.

Justin Allen: But those ordinary 99 percent people, with the (a) "me," they still have some kind of longing or some kind of underlying background seeking going on.

Andreas Müller: Oh, absolutely. There's seeking going on. Living in a belief system. Having clear values. Having goals. There's often a clear picture of good and bad; what would be nice. They don't dream about enlightenment. They dream about winning the lottery, or about their famous soccer club winning the cup, or stuff like that.

Justin Allen: But that kind of stuff, in general, would be unobservable. Like a spiritual teacher, from an outside view, it's obvious. It's obvious that there's a striving and there's a confirming of "the me."

Andreas Müller: No, I think it's equally obvious in those, what we define now as, ordinary lives. It's equally obvious.

Justin Allen: But how?

Andreas Müller: Oh, people tell it right away. What they want. What they think. That they have to do the work for the money and how they don't like it, and, "If I would only have more holidays." And, "If I would own an island," or, "If I would be so rich as that guy, if I would be Taylor Swift, that'll be great. But I have to sit here at the cash register in the super..."

Justin Allen: If you were a radar, if you had some kind of radar that could detect...

Andreas Müller: ...detect seeking? Oh, it's all around. Everywhere.

Justin Allen: Just in your apartment building here. Let's say somebody came through the apartment building and had a one-hour or a thirty-minute conversation with each apartment, you included. You don't know your other guests here, but let's just assume that they're all "me's" living (an) ordinary life like you. Do you think within a thirty-minute conversation that it'd be detectable that they are...

Andreas Müller: They might not notice a difference, but I guess they just wouldn't believe me if I say, "I don't care. Do you have plans? What are your plans for the next five years?" I think, as an entrepreneur, people would ask me, "Where do you see yourself in five years?" And I would just say, "Well, I don't care at all. I'm (blows air through lips) whatever." And the question would be, how would they process that? As me being crazy? As me being very cool? As lying? They may walk out the door and think, "Yeah, well, he does have some plans. I'm sure he wants more people. Come on." Stuff like that. So I think they just wouldn't believe me. They would take my answer personally and somehow process it. So they wouldn't notice.

Justin Allen: But planning also isn't necessarily proof that you're immune. You can also make…

Andreas Müller: Oh yeah, of course, my plans are on my website.

Justin Allen: But I mean, somebody would say, "What are your plans in five years?" And you would say, "I don't know, I'm just going to keep on doing what I'm doing, probably."

Andreas Müller: Absolutely. What people usually ask is, what do you want to achieve in those five years as a "me"? That's the actual question. They don't ask for my schedule. They ask, "What do you aim for?" and "What will bring you more fulfillment in five years?" They don't want to know what I cook tomorrow and what brings you joy…

Justin Allen: It's just reminding me of… do you know the movie, Blade Runner?

Andreas Müller: I know that it exists, but I haven't seen it.

Justin Allen: I think there are others like it. Somebody produced a bunch of AI that are identical to humans, and you can't distinguish. Harrison Ford has to go try to find one. And they do these tests. You have to do an interview with somebody. And through those tests, they try to find out if you're an actual human or…

Andreas Müller: No, the thing is that it's absolutely not hidden. Everyone who is a "me," they generally think that it's good to be "a me," which I don't think it's wrong, and that the values of the personal world are reality. So they constantly speak from that position, unconsciously. And, of course, they live in their value system and think that's how the world is, so they don't hide it. And I don't think it's bad either. I don't think they should hide it. But the same with the spiritual teachers. They just say openly that they are someone, unconsciously. They don't notice it. But this energy will just also be what it is, and it can't be hidden. That's why it would just take a few minutes, and you just kind of know if there is someone. Because they will speak from this position. And they can't do otherwise. That's also natural and not wrong. I think for most people, it would be clear in an instant or a few minutes when they talk about themselves, about their life. And, of course, for most people, seeking is just doing life, not seeking something deeper. They already, unconsciously, found an answer to their seeking. And the answer is, "Well, I just have to do life. It's my responsibility to earn money. It's my responsibility to have enough fun." They have already found a method for themselves that seems to work. "I'm the doer of my life."

Justin Allen: In talking about it in this way, we've heard things like, "The me dies," or "The me drops," or "The me collapses," or "The me falls away." Out of those options, or maybe a missing one, do you have a preferred way to...

Andreas Müller: Not really. What I like most is, it turns out to be non-existent. And its death is the turning out of its non-existence. None of those gets it, really. So they are all... (sighs) Because there was no "I" to drop. It's not that an illusion dropped here and... in one way it did, and in another way, it didn't at all because there was no illusion. And so on.

Justin Allen: Talking about it in all these various ways, it's not cryptic. Saying the "me" dies is cryptic. But it seems like it clouds something so simple. Potentially, if we're here, it makes it seem a little bit complicated.

Andreas Müller: Absolutely. I know.

Justin Allen: But that must be frustrating because it is very simple. Any way that you start to talk about it or try to describe it or communicate it, it gets muddy.

Andreas Müller: I know what you mean, but not really. Because the communication itself is also what we talk about. So I can say all those blurry and muddy things without having the impression that they are muddy. Because this sharing is exactly whole and complete. But I see how it's misunderstood and turned into something complicated, and I get that. And that is sometimes frustrating.

Justin Allen: You could interpret this in so many different ways.

Andreas Müller: Very often, in the end, it's just something like I say something, and afterward, we talk about how, "Oh, it wasn't meant like that. Oh no, that's not what I meant." Then I say something and then, "Ah, this means that," and I say, "No, it's not meant like that."

Justin Allen: Even the arc of our conversation, starting from 2020 or 2019, whenever we started, I could see when I would go back and read some things, I could also see how I was misinterpreting you. And then, sometimes, I could see I got it. And then sometimes I could see, even if I got what you were saying, then I might get confused again. Even in these conversations that we're having, I can see how it's not that different arguing with your partner or your friend or something like that, that somebody says something and they mean something else, or a text message. It's just funny how simple the message is that it would seem almost impossible. Because it isn't complicated.

Andreas Müller: Yeah, the mean thing with this is that it's not a message, even. So, it's neither complicated nor simple. It's not that there is a message in terms of I have one sentence. I have one truth.

Justin Allen: That's what I mean by so simple, is that it's not even a message.

Andreas Müller: Exactly.

Justin Allen: It's simpler than a message.

Andreas Müller: Exactly, it's just simpler. Exactly. (laughs) And again, it sounds cryptic and...

Justin Allen: Saying that it's simpler than a message already makes it seem...

Andreas Müller: ...out of range. Ungraspable.

Justin Allen: That's also how it starts to sound spiritual because we've been trained spiritually, and the greatest spiritual sentences are those kōan type things, somebody just takes a sentence and reverses... "It's not this, it's this." And then you're like, "Whoa!"

Andreas Müller: I know people who have a spiritual background, and they would call this the highest truth because it seems so out of range. It seems so far away.

Justin Allen: Rupert Spira, he will say, or people like him would say that that's the highest form. But then they'll critique it in a sense saying, but it's not very generous to the audience. It's too direct and it's like ripping off a bandaid instead of doing it gently. And he'll say, this is the gentle way or something like that.

Andreas Müller: (laughs) No, I think he totally rejects this message.

Justin Allen: I went to one of his meetings. And I think he did say that because there were people in the audience that referenced Tony Parsons.

Andreas Müller: Alright.

Justin Allen: And he had to address it, I think.

Andreas Müller: Okay.

Justin Allen: Maybe I'm wrong, but I think that's how he addressed it. He was differentiating himself, saying that there are very gentle ways of approaching this and there's more...

Andreas Müller: He'll have an answer, and he knows why his way is the better one.

Justin Allen: Another thing that I wanted to address. You have in your books photos with nature, don't you?

Andreas Müller: Not really.

Justin Allen: Well, like in your Instagram feed also, don't you have photos of nature a lot?

Andreas Müller: Yeah, I know. It should also be skyscrapers and piles of rubbish and... (both laugh) war zones, and empty wine bottles and whatever is regarded as not nice or industrial complexes, oil poisoning in the air. So, I know. (both laugh) I'm not very consequent in being a neutral, non-dual speaker. (laughs)

Justin Allen: I was thinking for the third book that maybe we should do a photo of trash instead of... in our books, we have paintings that I did. In the back, we always have an image.

Andreas Müller:	It feels a bit forced. (laughs) I'm fine with my pictures of nature.
	At least I don't download them from some picture page. They are pictures of my life and surroundings at least. And sometimes I'm in them. You see, I'm well aware of my shortcomings. My Instagram account with nice nature pictures is definitely one.
Justin Allen:	How long have you had the Instagram account?
Andreas Müller:	A bit more than a year, maybe. But to be honest, I had the idea to make a book out of them.
Justin Allen:	Out of the quotes?
Andreas Müller:	It's not only pictures and quotes. Usually, there's a short essay to the picture. And I had the idea at one point, I may even have a photo book with those pictures and the texts written.
Justin Allen:	And then, that would highlight what they thought was important or interesting?
Andreas Müller:	Mm hmm.
Justin Allen:	I thought that would be interesting. If you had enough of those types of...
Andreas Müller:	...highlighted....
Justin Allen:	Yeah, but not from you. Not things that you or I would select. If you had enough readers that selected things they liked, that would be interesting. And not a lot of work. (both laugh)
	In the past ten years, have you ever had any kind of serious health issue?
Andreas Müller:	No, I don't think so.

Justin Allen:	And no other kind of big tragedy or drama-type situation related to anything health-wise or family-wise or personal-wise?
Andreas Müller:	Not really. It depends on (laughs) what other people would regard as dramatic.
Justin Allen:	But from your point of view, no.
Andreas Müller:	No, it was all right. It was intense, but it was all right. But not health-wise. I'm fine. I think the biggest impact health-wise (was) when I had COVID, and it wasn't really bad, but it was intense. I didn't expect that.
Justin Allen:	As a way to try to compare how a "no me" would handle it, and how "a me" might handle it, how would you say, "This is how it is for a no me getting COVID and struggling with it for a little bit," and then, "this is what I imagine it would be like for a me that has COVID."
Andreas Müller:	To be honest, I can't say so. But the "me" would definitely know how it was for it. And I have no idea how it was for me. (laughs) So I can't really say anything about that.
Justin Allen:	But how would you imagine the inner dialogue, let's say?
Andreas Müller:	That's very individual, because every "me," has their own approach to life.
Justin Allen:	Yeah, but just one that you could imagine that might be an inner dialogue for "a me."
Andreas Müller:	I don't know. "Why did it happen to me? I should have worn a mask. What? I am vaccinated" or, "I should have vaccinated myself," or... it would somehow dance around itself.

Justin Allen:	For you, when you had COVID, what would be the inner thought?
Andreas Müller:	There was no dialogue, really.
Justin Allen:	But it might be like, "This is worse than I thought it would be."
Andreas Müller:	Oh yeah, that's... (both laugh) that's a thought that came up. Maybe it could even be the same thoughts. But it wouldn't be a dialogue. It would just be the brain producing thoughts for "no one," and I can't say how that is. But those thoughts would just never become my reality. In terms of, it is really like that for me, and I really miss important things. And if I were healthy, it would be much nicer, which for the person means I would be closer to being fulfilled. It just can't be described how it is when that's "no me" there.
Justin Allen:	But if we took your sentence where you said when you had COVID, "Whoa, this is worse than I thought it was going to be." And let's say that "a me" had that same thought. So you both have COVID, and you're both shocked that it's this bad. Then all you could say is that energetically if you were trying to make a distinction between... even though you're sharing the same type of inner thought and dialogue as "a me..."
Andreas Müller:	The problem really with that is that that distinction isn't real.
Justin Allen:	But if you were trying to explain it, wouldn't it just be like, there's an energetic difference to the inner dialogue that "a me" has than...
Andreas Müller:	Only apparently, but not really. (You wouldn't) be able to put your finger on it and say, "That's the difference between being me and between not be-

ing me." Or you just put the finger, so to speak, on the me illusion, because that's the only difference. There isn't another difference.

Justin Allen: If I was trying to make a distinction, I might speculate that that's the brain making that thought, "Oh, this is worse than I thought it was going to be." Whereas "the me" wouldn't be distinguishing it as a thought. It would be feeling it very deeply, like, "It's happening to me."

Andreas Müller: Exactly, that's what I mean. It would somehow live to be in that situation and to live in that story that the brain comes up with or that it tells itself. That would be its truth and its reality.

Justin Allen: There could be "a me" that has the thought, "This is worse than I thought it was." So there's one "me" that has that thought, and there could be another "me" that has the same thought. For one, it could be much more emotionally intense. And for the other one, it's a little bit less emotionally intense. But still, it's felt fundamentally and deeply that...

Andreas Müller: ...that it's personal. That it's real. That it's a real happening...

Justin Allen: ...that even COVID is something separate that you get. It happens to you and it's destroying your body and giving you symptoms.

Andreas Müller: Exactly, and of course, the whole energy of seeking would be attached to it. This whole idea of, "I have a life, and this is a part of my life now, and it's about something else," where having COVID, on the other hand, becomes something very small. It may seem huge, but on the other hand, it would just be part of something much greater, namely my life and my path toward something. And this energy would just be attached to it, where it can't be seen anymore that having COVID and having thoughts about COVID is the natural, complete, and whole reality.

Justin Allen: And for a person where there's "no me," then you could be having "thoughts" like, "Wow, this is worse than I thought it would be." But it wouldn't be a chapter in a book of your life.

Andreas Müller: Exactly.

Justin Allen: And it wouldn't be felt in the way that "a me" knows how it's felt.

Andreas Müller: It would just feel like that.

Justin Allen: For you, it would be more like how you also picked up a glass of water in the day and drank it. And you might have had a thought when you drank the water like, "Oh, water tastes good."

Andreas Müller: It would just be what seems to be happening and wouldn't have, in that sense, a deeper meaning.

Justin Allen: It would be as insignificant or as significant as earlier in the day when you drank the water. Whereas, in a "me" scenario, the dilemma with COVID is on a hierarchy. On that day, that person had COVID; they didn't even remember drinking the water, and the water was so insignificant.

Andreas Müller: The question usually is, how much does this impact my path? How much does what happens, in a good or in a bad way, impact my path toward fulfillment? And, of course, the bigger the impact is on my path toward fulfillment, the more important it is. So, when I had plans to have an enlightenment seminar this week, I got COVID, and I couldn't participate then this seems to have had a huge impact on my path towards enlightenment. Very simplified. That's how the person would see it. "Oh, that's where those ideas of meaning come from, and importance."

Justin Allen: Even though "a me" is essentially there the entire time.

Andreas Müller: Even?

Justin Allen: This "me" feeling or this "me" awareness.

Andreas Müller: Doesn't have to, no one knows...

Justin Allen: But it's there all the time, in the sense that if there's "a me, " there's "a me."

Andreas Müller: When there is this illusion running, then yes.

Justin Allen: But we've talked about this also in previous books. You can imagine in the 24-hour day of "a me" life that there are periods when there's just no inner dialogue and no story and no feeling that I'm here living with my story.

Andreas Müller: Yeah.

Justin Allen: But the "me" can't use that as a reference because for it to be doing that, it's there. So it's negated that possibility.

Andreas Müller: Yeah.

Justin Allen: That's kind of what you're saying, is the life that you live is that chunk; that "me's" not there, but all the time.

Andreas Müller: In a very simplified picture.

Justin Allen: I said this in one of the previous talks we had, but that's the only way...

Andreas Müller: ...it can be processed or understood, and that I'm in a continuous state of not being "a me," which is a total dream. That's not what I'm saying. Sorry, I have to point this out. But that's how it's usually regarded. "Oh, Andreas, he's liberated," as if something like that exists and as if it's an ongoing state. Then, when I say it's not an ongoing state, the person would say, "Ah, so the me is coming and going for you." No no.

Justin Allen: No, it's just never there.

Andreas Müller: There just isn't anyone. And that's not a circumstance in a real world, in an ongoing reality. But, again, I guess it starts to sound cryptic. Or that's how the seeker would see it.

Justin Allen: Fantastical, maybe. Cryptic always is a little bit dark.

Andreas Müller: Yeah. Mystical. Cryptical..

Justin Allen: It's asked often, or people want to know what it's like for you to not be there. But I get the dilemma. It is such a simple thing too. You can't say it's a realization. You can't say that it's something that you figured out. You can't say that you just see it, that it's like a seeing. You can't say it's a feeling. Supposedly, we have five or six senses, and that's how we have to navigate the world. And so we have to understand the world with those senses. And that's how we make sense of anything.

Andreas Müller: I'm just doubting if we make sense of the world with our senses. But I think the senses just function, and in that sense, maybe make sense of the world. But this inner feeling of, "Oh, this makes sense, and this makes sense to me..."

Justin Allen: Yeah, that has nothing to do with the senses.

Andreas Müller: Exactly. Yeah, alright.

Justin Allen: But that is a good point. The sense of the "me," also falls out of our biological understanding of the world. And people like to invent senses, also. The sixth sense, and then they would come up with a seventh sense when you realize you're not there. (both laugh)

Andreas Müller: The sentence is already... it's such a contradiction, and it doesn't exist: "I'm not there anymore." There's nothing here that lives in a narrative about itself. There's just really no narrative going on here. So I don't tell myself that there is "no me" or that there isn't anyone or stuff like that.

Justin Allen: It just is that way.

Andreas Müller: It just is that way.

Justin Allen: And then somebody goes, "But how do you know it's that way or why is it that way?" But you still try to describe it or...

Andreas Müller: Yeah. But of course, when I say, "It just is that way," the person again assumes that it's a circumstance, and all it can understand is, "Okay, but you must know that." Well, no. There is "no one."

Justin Allen: When you do tell your story, a two-year process of fading away, and then you weren't there anymore at some point, and then you recognize it, that you were never there. It's not possible to define that, describe it, or explain it in any way.

Andreas Müller: It is impossible.

Justin Allen: It would be nice if there would be one way where you could say, you realize that you're not there, but it's not intellectual. It's not a feeling. It's not this, it's not that, but it doesn't do that justice either.

Andreas Müller:	Because again, the person would be left with the impression, "Okay, it's not this, it's not this, it's not this, it's not this. But it must be something, and I just can't grasp it." So there's just no way out.
Justin Allen:	Even with your Instagram thing, there's an image of a tree (both laugh) and then there's a sentence. If you click then there might be a longer text. But you're pulling those from where?
Andreas Müller:	I write them new.
Justin Allen:	You might be sitting here at the computer, and then you think of something to write.
Andreas Müller:	Exactly.
Justin Allen:	Ah, I thought you were pulling them from your books or talks.
Andreas Müller:	Only 5 or 10 percent. Sometimes, if there's nothing there, I take something from a book. But mostly I write them freshly. Sometimes an idea lingers on from a Zoom that I had, or... I think that's where it comes from.
Justin Allen:	But it's kind of like if I'm a poet, all of a sudden I have an idea and I get inspired and I write a poem.
Andreas Müller:	It is like that.
Justin Allen:	Yeah. Okay. Well, that's different, then. Let's say there's a dilemma of communicating this to a person. The dilemma is only there because of all the questions that you get, and you have an understanding of how difficult this is to grasp from a me-point perspective. But did, then, you ever think, " Oh, maybe this is another way to..."
Andreas Müller:	I think the communication is perfect. I'm sorry.

Justin Allen:	I'm not saying that it's flawed, but still, you do have different ways. You don't have one way of communicating it.
Andreas Müller:	Yeah, but again, it's not choosing. It's the words that are coming out, and I think they are perfect.
Justin Allen:	But you haven't stopped. You have additional words that you're using, and additional paragraphs, and additional configurations of words.
Andreas Müller:	Absolutely, oh yeah, of course. There's no standstill, but yeah.
Justin Allen:	But that was my question, do you ever come up with a different configuration of how to communicate, for example, what it's like?
Andreas Müller:	Only out of the conversation, so it's not that I think about it. But there are things that I would say nowadays, and there might be things in five years where I wouldn't say it anymore like I say it now. But my impression is it's rather a change than a development because sometimes I say things again that I said five years ago for the last time.
Justin Allen:	Do you ever think metaphorically sometimes that you see something happen in nature or on the street, like a car driving by?
Andreas Müller:	Hmm, no.
Justin Allen:	Do you ever read a book and there's something in there that makes you say, "Oh, I could relate this to my talks."
Andreas Müller:	Maybe sometimes. All of that is what seems to be happening. So, I'm not consciously doing that. Maybe that's why I can't remember. Of course, sometimes I hear a sentence that I like that was

completely meant in a different way from where I heard it, but I could apply it to this.

Justin Allen: I come up with questions sometimes because I read something and then I think, maybe it's an interesting thing to ask, or this is a comparison.

Andreas Müller: Yes, sometimes.

Justin Allen: But you're not actively trying to say, "How could I figure this out…"

Andreas Müller: Oh, not at all. I'm not saying anything, and I'm not trying to bring across a message. So I don't feel any dilemma, even. I don't feel this dilemma of, "Eh, it's so simple, but I can't bring it across," because I don't want to bring something across. Not even how simple it is, which "it" should be, which is simple, so to speak. So I don't feel any dilemma with that. I have someone, it's funny we talked about it already, but he's almost constantly saying (to) me that I'm using the wrong words because he doesn't get it. So he's constantly making me wrong, so to speak. "You are explaining it wrong, and others explain it much better, and if you would do…" I don't have that. Oh, that's maybe how Tony would say it: it's just purely energetic, this apparent dynamic between the seeker and "no one." But there's nothing here; I don't feel… that's why I can't work on (a) presentation because it's just coming out so directly.

Justin Allen: But that's true also of anybody, no?

Andreas Müller: Of course.

Justin Allen: The only difference would be that somebody might think that they're actively working on it.

Andreas Müller: That's true. They would have the illusion of actively working on it, yeah. But this might also be, then, what seems to be happening. I don't know that people sit down and think about, "How can I make this more approachable or understandable?" I don't know.

Justin Allen: But even in those cases, that's not "the me" actively sitting down trying to figure it out. But the experience of it is that.

Andreas Müller: Exactly. But all of that would just be what seems to be happening.

Justin Allen: But having a quote that you put onto Instagram. Maybe it happens, you're just sitting down, or you just got done with the Zoom conversation. Even earlier today in this talk, you said something, and then I was like, "Okay, so we figured that out." And then you go, "But I haven't," and then you wanted to add something. You continued with some kind of thought that you had during the Zoom and you thought, "Oh, I want to share this."

Andreas Müller: Exactly.

Justin Allen: Let's say that "a me," somebody that thinks that they're there, also gave a lecture or a talk. And then later on, they wanted to expand on it. They would do it as well. But for them, it might be a struggle or a dilemma.

Andreas Müller: Maybe a struggle or a need to express it, as if it wasn't complete before. Maybe a need to clarify things or...

Justin Allen: It would also feel like a choice. And even if it didn't feel like a choice, if they felt like, "I don't even have a choice that I'm writing this. It's just..."

Andreas Müller: "I had to write this."

Justin Allen: Yeah, it's still underlying all that, that there's a tone of...

Andreas Müller: ...need.

Justin Allen: Somebody being there having to do something or
                         not.

Andreas Müller: Out of the need.

Justin Allen: In that case, they could think that it's not a need.
                         They could just be very convinced that it's almost
                         something that they just have to get out.

Andreas Müller: Yeah, but that's the need: "Something I had to get
                         out."

Justin Allen: True.

Andreas Müller: For whatever reason. But I don't want to express
                         myself in those texts or those presentations.

Justin Allen: If you were trying to answer why you're doing it; if
                         you were being authentic about it, you wouldn't be
                         able to answer.

Andreas Müller: Yeah.

Justin Allen: And if you were to answer, then it would just be...

Andreas Müller: There is "no one."

Justin Allen: Right now, I'm at a point in this conversation where
                         I almost can't continue, you know? It's almost like
                         I'm... (both laugh) sitting here, struggling to create
                         content for us to talk about, but it's okay. It doesn't
                         matter. In general, somebody is always trying to ex-
                         press themselves in some way.

Andreas Müller:	Yes, exactly.
Justin Allen:	The absence of trying to express yourself, but still apparently expressing yourself, that's also something that you can't get. But somehow I think when you were younger, or at least for me, it seemed like there was a sense of, that you did things without being there.
Andreas Müller:	Maybe, as a child, I say yes.
Justin Allen:	If you were to go running for your health, and you started to feel some kind of pain, it seems typical that an adult will continue to run. Let's just assume that scenario. There, of course, will be people that stop, but let's say the adult continues to run. And then the pain doesn't go away, but you can ignore it, more or less. And then you go to the doctor's, and the doctor says that you tore your ACL in your knee, or you have tendonitis or something. And then the doctor says you have to do these exercises and relax or take a break from running. And then the doctor also points out, "You know, I noticed this. There's a difference between adults and children. When a child runs, if they were going jogging and their knee hurt or they had some kind of pain, they would stop running. But an adult won't, because an adult thinks that they can work through the pain or that they just have to keep on continuing." When I was a child, I wasn't aware of things that I had to do or how I had to behave. When I was doing things, it was like I wasn't aware of what I was doing. It was just...
Andreas Müller:	...happening.
Justin Allen:	Yeah. As an adult or even from a teenage year, then there was a dialogue, and there was an awareness of I'm doing this and a feeling like I have to do this, or responsibility to myself and the world. And I

think of that as a good example that there's "a me," or in this case, an adult is motivated by an inner...

Andreas Müller: ...in a conflict, oh absolutely. But I don't know if that's an adult or if it's "the me."

Justin Allen: It's a dilemma because, in that situation where you're running, there's an inner dialogue already going, "I should probably stop because my body hurts."

Andreas Müller: Exactly. And there would be a fight between seemingly contradictory values.

Justin Allen: For the child, it would just be easy. I just stop. And there's no punishment. Whereas for the adult, there's a punishment because the adult thinks, "I have to run 30 minutes every day to stay thin and fit and healthy. And if I stop I'm weak. I'm giving in to the pain."

Andreas Müller: But to be honest, I would say it's a "me" thing. It's not an adult-child thing. But I understand for most people in childhood, "the me" just sneaks in or is there and isn't there. But also, when I see a young child playing soccer, which I do at times nowadays, this kind of conflict can already happen. But they aren't "a me" as strongly and as often as adults are. Let's put it like this.

Justin Allen: But that inner conflict... it could also happen to you that you go jogging and you get knee pain, but you continue to jog. But you wouldn't have...

Andreas Müller: There wouldn't be someone in a conflict. Absolutely.

Justin Allen: "The me" situation where there is this inner conflict, you can see how confusing it is for this person, just by the nature of the conflict: should I continue running or shouldn't I continue running?

Andreas Müller: Yeah, is there a better and a worse? Again, what is more fulfilling, what has a greater impact on my path, and what's more?

Justin Allen: It wants out of the conflict and it wants to know...

Andreas Müller: ...what's better and not? And it can't because there is no better and worse.

Justin Allen: Yeah, who's going to answer? Because even in that case, if you just take jogging and, "Should I stop or should I continue," you want to trust yourself. But how can you know which of those two is yourself? And then, on top of that, you have the inner dialogue from all the shit that you've heard your whole life, which is like the doctor that says, "Follow your body. Listen to your body." And then somebody else says, "No, listen to your mind." And then somebody says, "Listen to your heart." Somebody says, "Listen to your gut."

Andreas Müller: Exactly. Trust yourself.

Justin Allen: Yeah. You can think in your life, "Ahh yeah, I should listen to my body. Cause last time I didn't, I listened to my mind, and I ended up tearing the joint in my knee." And then you go, "Oh no, but I shouldn't just listen to my body because there was that time that I listened to my body, and I ended up doing this terrible thing."

Andreas Müller: Yeah. That's the utter confusion the person seems to live in. And in a way, I think for most people, that's an ongoing experience. One could say "the me" is constantly in this dilemma because it's constantly in this situation that what happens is different from its story about what happens. Because the person lives in a real world where everything is real, and that's just not the case. So it constantly lives in this artificial contradiction, that it thinks I'm experiencing a real world, but it just isn't real. Of course, it's unconscious of that contradiction. But in a way, that's the tension the person constantly lives in. But then it starts seeking those details, so to speak, in the real world, in terms of "Should I seek? Should I listen to the heart? Is the guru right? No, I don't believe in gurus. I only trust myself." Or "I only trust what my mother told me."

Justin Allen: Yeah.

Andreas Müller: It's such a desperate way to find orientation, and it doesn't work because it's a completely illusory world.

Justin Allen: And there's no orientation.

Andreas Müller: And there is no orientation, and there is "no one" who is on a path who needs orientation. Exactly.

Justin Allen: But "the me" in that situation wants there to be a point of orientation, and that's really what they think that they're seeking, is finding...

Andreas Müller: ...comfort. Be safe.

Justin Allen: Yeah, but also their true self in a way so that when they meet future conflicts, they have one strong center that can guide them. And they think that that's what you have or what a guru has.

Andreas Müller: Absolutely.

Justin Allen: Let's just say that there is "no me" for children until five years old, and it happens. Within those five years, children also make "mistakes" and "bad choices." And they get diseases and break their legs. And so it also doesn't mean that if "the me" drops, all of a sudden you live a perfect life where when your knee hurts, you always stop at the right moment and when...

Andreas Müller:	Exactly. It turns out that the life that's being lived is perfect as it is, but it doesn't become perfect in a sense like, I'll never break my leg. Life will just be as life is, which is the perfect life.
Justin Allen:	And it already is a perfect life running with the feeling like there's "a me" there that needs to decide, "should I stop or should I go on."
Andreas Müller:	This too, yeah.
Justin Allen:	That's also the perfect life.
Andreas Müller:	In a way, yes.
Justin Allen:	And that's a perfect life because that's still...
Andreas Müller:	It's what seems to be happening.
Justin Allen:	Yeah. In that case, it seems to be that there's "a me" happening that's having these inner dialogues. And if, in that instance, "me" drops, maybe running continues, and maybe it stops. But it won't be because of "a me" struggling and making a decision.
Andreas Müller:	Exactly, and it wouldn't need to serve "a me," neither the running nor the stopping at the right moment. Because, of course, that's what "the me" wants from this. It wants, "Yeah, this serves me; what happens, or how my body is, or how my reactions are; that they serve me."
Justin Allen:	And you, if you're running and you stop, it wouldn't be for any reason, really. It wouldn't be because your knee hurts.
Andreas Müller:	No, it would only be because the knee hurts, but not because I think that that's bad for me, as on my path towards fulfillment when the knee hurts. Yeah. It would just be stopping because the knee hurts.

Justin Allen:	Maybe, or you might continue with the knee pain.
Andreas Müller:	And there is never a real knowing why, because this whole happening isn't real, as such.
Justin Allen:	But when "a me" is running and "the me" stops because "the me" thinks that it's choosing to stop in order not to damage their knee further or something like that...
Andreas Müller:	... to not lose fulfillment. It's also the person who doesn't really care about if the knee is damaged or not. The personal question is, "What's the impact," again, "on my path towards fulfillment if my knee is hurt?" That's why there is this inner dialogue.
Justin Allen:	That's the broader unconscious picture. But in the moment that they're running, if you make it that simple as, "Should I continue running or not," "the me" thinks that it's making a choice. In that case, if it made a choice to stop running, and then I met a doctor the next day, and the doctor said, "Good thing you stopped running because I did an MRI, and I could see that if you had taken one more bounce, you would have..."
Andreas Müller:	Exactly. And "the me" would say, "I don't want to have a hurt knee. Of course, I stopped running."
Justin Allen:	Well, then "the me" would feel verified. "Wow, I made the right choice. I'm so happy."
Andreas Müller:	"Good that I am. Without me, I wouldn't have stopped running. Because who would have taken that decision? Without me, I'm sure I would have a broken knee now."
Justin Allen:	And that's also the dilemma, when "a me" hears this message of not being "a me," that it would use that example as, "who would then decide..."

Andreas Müller: Absolutely.

Justin Allen: And the fear would be, if "the me" wasn't there, then I might have just kept on running and I would have damaged my knee permanently.

Andreas Müller: Exactly. "And this would be bad."

Justin Allen: "The me" still thinks that what happens is that when "the me" drops, somehow, it always makes the right decision without conflict.

Andreas Müller: Which, in a way, is like that because every decision in that sense is whole and complete and is the right decision, but it has nothing to do with the ideas of the person, the right outcome. Because for the person, the right decision is always connected to the outcome of that decision, and the need for a certain outcome just drops when the person drops, and in that sense, every decision is the right one; not in a holy spiritual way because it can also be what we would regard as the wrong decision. But this narrative completely drops, actually, about right or wrong in that sense.

Justin Allen: If "the me" is aware that there's "a me," and sees that as a problem in its life, that there's a... at some point, "the me" might be like, "Fuck. I'm in such a conflict because every time I have to make a decision, there seems to be multiple me's." There's "the me" that says to keep running. And then there's "the me" that says stop running. And then there's the "third me" that's aware of "the me" that's saying to keep on running, and "the me" that's saying to stop running. And it's all like, which "me" should I trust? And then which one isn't there? It thinks, though, that enlightenment or "the me" dying type of thing leaves them with some simpler way of living life without this conflict, in whatever form that's imagined.

Andreas Müller: Yes.

Justin Allen: And then, they also speculate that when that happens, life will go on much more simply.

Andreas Müller: Yes. But for "me." All for "me."

Justin Allen: The outcome is that they imagine that it's not gonna be this terrible struggle anymore, and they think that they will make better decisions now in the next 20 years than they had been making before.

Andreas Müller: Exactly. And they'll be able to collect more and more fulfillment and happiness by making the right decisions.

Justin Allen: The previous 20 years, they made all these mistakes, and then, now they're enlightened, or "the me" has dropped for them. I'm not saying that those are two equal things. I'm saying Enlightenment is one thing, and "the me" dropping is another thing. But in either case, for them, it means the same thing.

Andreas Müller: Exactly. Namely that I can be here and go on living without the need to seek; without struggle.

Justin Allen: Let's say that they think that they're enlightened or that "the me" has dropped. Even if it really has, for them, still, as they're imagining the next 20 years, they would be saying, "These are going to be good," no matter what, because there's no longer this conflict. And those past 20 years, all those mistakes that happened were because of "the me."

Andreas Müller: Yeah.

Justin Allen: And that's something that I wanted to point out is that it's not because of "the me," ever.

Andreas Müller: Yes, exactly. Because it's an illusion that there was "me," that there ever was a real autonomous thing that was separate and had an influence, ever.

Justin Allen: So even in the case where there is "a me," and there's no enlightenment, they think that there's something there making the good decision or the bad decision, or the middle decision. And then, at some point, if that were to be removed, they would go on, "making mistakes" and "making good decisions."

Andreas Müller: Yes.

Justin Allen: But it would no longer feel that way, that they're the ones making the bad decision. And there wouldn't be a regret or a reward like, "Wow, I, did right by myself."

Andreas Müller: Yes. This would all just collapse and turn out to have never been the case. Regret. Reward. Guide. Guilt and pride.

Justin Allen: You say often also that there's no difference. That's why life is also so ordinary. It's because life is going to be, no matter what, in parentheses, bad and good and unavoidable, making mistakes or getting cancer or winning the lottery or getting the promotion or something like that. It's all not because of you.

Andreas Müller: Exactly. Already for anyone.

Justin Allen: In either case, if we say that you're not there but I'm here, we're both going to go on in one week from now. And then one week from now, we will have done whatever things, and I will have felt that I did the right things or the wrong things, and you will not...

Andreas Müller:

...and live in a narrative with yourself about yourself and the dialogue. But that's also unchosen. No one chose this. It's also the natural and impersonal reality.

Justin Allen:

I was talking to a friend, and I won't be able to paraphrase our conversation that well, but he seemed to be grasping or to have understood that this message is communicating that there's just "no one" there. And he was saying, "Well, although I feel like I understand that, that there's no one there, of course, I can't fundamentally grasp that. But I still am going to go on with my life." He was saying, "Maybe I'm going to start this business, or maybe I decide I want to travel in my van across Africa. And I know that I'm doing it because of this me, but I can't stop myself. And I don't know if it's the right thing, or what if the me wasn't there, and I would be happy with my current circumstances. But right now, I just feel like, unavoidably, out of my control, I'm guided by this me force that's going to either do this or is going to do that. And even if there's a part of me that doesn't want to, that says, 'Why are you still trying to do all these things when they don't bring you anything? There's no reward. There's nothing happening,' but I can't stop myself." And he's going, "Anything I do or how I feel, it's out of my grasp. And I'm just gonna end up doing it even if part of me is saying not to. There's also nothing I can do to improve myself." And he's like, "I guess, maybe, the me will drop at some point." Right? This is a sentence that you hear also, no? But then he goes, "But there's nothing I can do to make the me drop. It's either going to, or it's not. Or, it's not even there right now." He's saying this kind of stuff. And that's an understanding.

Andreas Müller:

Absolutely. It's an apparent understanding.

Justin Allen:

It's an apparent understanding. But still, some people get this message, and some people don't get the message. When people get your message, it doesn't mean that they're not there.

Andreas Müller: Yeah.

Justin Allen: And some people don't get the message, and those would be people that think you're a spiritual teacher, still, and giving them advice. Those people just don't get what you're saying. Then, some people get what you're saying...

Andreas Müller: Apparently. (laughs)

Justin Allen: Apparently, but some people don't feel like you're teaching them, and don't feel like you're giving them advice, or telling them what to do, or that there's something that they can do. And those are usually the people...

Andreas Müller: ...that come.

Justin Allen: Yeah. And that also feel a little bit more relaxed about...

Andreas Müller: Absolutely, but also can unconsciously sense the relief that's coming from this message.

Justin Allen: They don't seem to be so neurotic and wrapped up in trying to alleviate things or correct things. But in that case, even when somebody gets that message, it seems to me that there's something energetically that's changed within them as well, to the point where there's nothing more they're going to get from you.

Andreas Müller: ...to think about, or it's the end of the concept. You can't add any more to the concept.

Justin Allen: And then even knowing that that hasn't brought them anything. They're truly at the end of the rope or at the end of the line.

Andreas Müller: They are at the end of the thought stream.

Justin Allen: Yeah. That's what you feel like is the end of the line because...

Andreas Müller: Exactly. That's how it feels for them. "Okay. I can't go further with this information."

Justin Allen: They're at an intellectual dead end. They're at a psychological dead end, essentially. At this point, anytime that they start grabbing for something, it's empty now. And so, for that person, they can't confirm themselves anymore, either.

Andreas Müller: I wouldn't say so. Because in this whole process, they are constantly confirming themselves energetically.

Justin Allen: Okay, but don't you think that there is something else that's not quite awareness, but something that's...

Andreas Müller: I don't think so. I think it's just from this point on, there could either this or this happen I mean, a lot of people at this moment, they just put aside the message and go on with their life and seek in whatever they seek in. I think that happens a lot. That happens a lot to partners of people who come to this message; they just instantly get the concept and say, "Okay, I got it," and then they just go on seeking whatever they seek. It's never completely understood. The basic ideas are formed into a concept that seems to make sense to them. And they say, "Okay, there is no one. I can't do anything." And then they go on seeking. And it doesn't, in that sense, have hardly any or no impact on their personal energy at all. But those don't come anymore.

But then there could also be that there's just an energetic resonance from this point on and an adventurous interest of, "Oh, wow, I can't grasp this intellectually at all. But there is something." All of this wouldn't be conscious. In that sense, it could go both ways, but it doesn't necessarily have to be that it has an impact on the sense of "I am" just because you thought it through.

Justin Allen: But do you think the people that start, that there are several people that are also like my friend, in this case?

Andreas Müller: Then they would teach this message.

Justin Allen: Yeah, I know, but they wouldn't think that they're teaching this message.

Andreas Müller: They wouldn't think that they are teaching something, but they would be teaching something.

Justin Allen: But do you think that's the case of the people that sometimes pop up on YouTube?

Andreas Müller: Absolutely, a hundred percent, yeah. I think, just as some people get high on understanding concepts, you can also get high on understanding this concept because it seems to provide very simple answers to all the problems of life. And you can get high on that for half a year until life proves the opposite; that it's not as easy and simple as the concepts are; that it's not a simple reality in terms of, it's real and it follows one simple principle. No. It's wild. It's nothing, and it can't be grasped at all. That's why they are usually also gone after half a year, or a year, or one and a half years. Because, again, their own experience, or what they believe, contradicts what life is doing.

Justin Allen: But do you think that there's also those people that are convinced, at that point that, they're identical to you in a sense?

Andreas Müller: Yeah.

Justin Allen: And that they think also that that's what happened to you is that you got to that point, and then once you got to that point, you could communicate this message.

Andreas Müller: Exactly. And they think that I'm doing the same, yeah. That's the only way "the me" can comprehend this. As we talked about, that's what most people think, that I am someone who has somehow come to this experience. And, of course, for many people, to come to this experience means to understand it. So, yeah, they think that's what happens here, and that's what they think. They can do it, too.

Justin Allen: Yeah, that would be a way to... a scientist is running some experiment, and because of the results of this experiment, based on that understanding and seeing it, they can say, "Oh, therefore, life means this." Whereas somebody else maybe doesn't intellectually grasp what happened.

Andreas Müller: I don't know how conscious or unconscious that is. When that happens, the one person thinks that I'm fulfilled now. They get high on this understanding and think that they are fulfilled now. And they attach their ideas to what being fulfilled means. As long as there is someone, life will prove the opposite. There is no fulfilled me. So after a while, they just notice that they aren't. Or something happens that they can't include in their concept of what being enlightened means.

I've heard this story a few times that people were teaching, and then something was happening to them that they thought could never happen to them, or which they thought they would react to that, much more enlightened. A separation. A divorce. A disease. Or trauma coming up. And they thought for 20 or 30 years that this couldn't happen to them because they were enlightened. Or how much they were shocked, or how deeply impacted their experience, and then they stopped teaching. That's what I mean: sooner or later, there might be something that contradicts their own story about it. And I think with understanding it is quite easy. If people base their idea of being enlightened just purely on understanding, it's very easy for something to happen that contradicts that. But it's just a story. I have no idea. I'm just saying it's my impression.

Justin Allen: It's like a subtle trick that you could genuinely feel like you figured it out.

Andreas Müller: Oh, totally. It's an experience that "the me" constantly has. It's constantly dealing with problems and constantly comes up with an idea and has the impression, "I figured that out."

Justin Allen: This would be a bigger event, in a way.

Andreas Müller: Exactly. But usually, also in those small things, life proves the opposite. But how often do people think, "Oh, great! That's how my relationship works," or "Ah, now I figured out why..."

Justin Allen: Yeah, that happens all the time.

Andreas Müller: That's what I mean. It's just a very common personal experience.

Justin Allen: Those are so common that they don't feel super... in the context of spirituality, but even more so in the case of the message that you're communicating, it's rarer. First of all, there are not so many of you. None of you have a super large audience.

Andreas Müller: Absolutely.

Justin Allen: Because already, to get to the point where some-body's listening to you in general, they might have already gone through a bunch of life...

Andreas Müller: Sorry, this is a story as well, of course, and I have no idea. But the interesting thing is that this started (referring to people "teaching" this sort of message online) during the pandemic when there were a lot of Zooms and online stuff. So there are a lot of peo-ple right now who started all these things, who have never or hardly been to an actual meeting with Tony or Jim or me. They just had a lot of videos.

Justin Allen: You're saying, in this case, that there are people that have seen videos and then felt like, "Ahh, I figured it out."

Andreas Müller: That's how it seems to me, but I have no idea.

Justin Allen: With spiritual enlightenment from teachers, the way that it kind of feels, if you were enlightened, is that you had some kind of a big moment. At least, that's my imagining of it. So, for me to have ever been tricked into thinking that I was enlightened, it meant that there would have had to have been some kind of event that was indisputable; that all of a sudden I'm transformed, and I'm...

Andreas Müller: Maybe, so far. Maybe then someone else would tell you that there is no such event; that enlightenment is subtle and sneaks in and...

Justin Allen: Yeah, maybe. But I'm saying that's what it was for me. So, for me to be a spiritual teacher like Ady-ashanti or Rupert Spira or Eckhart Tolle, I would have had to have felt like how somebody feels when they take LSD or mushrooms or something, where they have a huge epiphany that transforms their whole perception of life, and then they can be like, "Wow, I'm no longer... I have to give myself a new name. And it's going to be something that nobody recognized before." (both laugh) Or, "I have to start wearing new clothes. I have to totally..."

Andreas Müller: I'm new. I've become someone new.

Justin Allen: Yeah, exactly. That's what I imagined happened to X, Y, and Z people. With your message, though, first of all, there's not a big history behind it. With spiritual teaching, there is a long history of it. With this message, it's relatively new, or at least it's new to the audience that's currently listening to it. And then all the people that are communicating the message don't seem otherworldly. Whereas, spiritual teachers kind of seem otherworldly, like how Prince, the musician, seems otherworldly. And even he puts on a costume; he has an entourage; he has an aura about him; and he acts weird in interviews.

Andreas Müller: And it's also kind of created.

Justin Allen: And that makes sense that he would create that because he's performing... he's putting on a show. But nobody in this message is performing or putting on a show or anything like that. So it just seems like it would be relatively easy in a way because to go from me to Eckhart Tolle seems like a big leap, but for me to go to you doesn't seem like a big leap.

Andreas Müller: Yes. Anyone can do it. (both laugh) Which is kind of true, and also not.

Justin Allen: That goes back to what you were saying, during COVID. All you need to do is make a YouTube video and communicate similar sentences.

Andreas Müller: Exactly.

Justin Allen: And it seems like that's a legitimate thing. Whereas, if you were trying to be Rupert Spira on a YouTube video, it's very difficult because you don't have the entourage and the show and the performance and all the things that you (see) behind it. So nobody's going to be drawn into it or believe it... "What have you done? You haven't gone and lived in India yet for 10 years and done whatever you need to do to be the enlightened person."

Andreas Müller: You don't have a shiny disclaimer. Yep. True.

HALF-TALK

Justin Allen:

We're here again in your apartment. (both laugh) And the talk that we had previously, I was running out of things to talk about. But I thought about that. There may be a certain drive that somebody has to figure things out outside of even this message.

I just thought I'd summarize what we've done. When we first started talking in 2019 or 2020, I had an idea in my head. Originally, I wasn't expecting to talk to you or your message because I interpreted your message differently than what was intended. Maybe. Not that I was seeking enlightenment from you, but the initial thing for me was, "What is enlightenment?" And I wanted somebody to prove that they were enlightened, or that enlightenment was possible, or at least that it's just all bullshit (or not).

You were the person who agreed to talk with me about it (I had contacted Mooji, Adyashanti, Rupert Spira, and Eckart Tolle, to name a few), and very quickly, you communicated, "Hey, you're not gonna get enlightened from talking to me." (both laugh) And, whether it's quickly or not, it became clear: okay, that settled enlightenment for me a little bit. Through our talks, at least. Whether I felt secure or not, this search for enlightenment or figuring it all out dropped or wasn't there. And then the energy that took over when we were talking was more in tune with this idea of "no me."

Andreas Müller:	All right.
Justin Allen:	And so that's continued because, if you're coming to you intending to figure something out, there's a quick (hits hand against the wall) dead end or wall that you're gonna face. So, how many times can you keep on knocking on the door or running up against the wall?
Andreas Müller:	Yeah.
Justin Allen:	Our talks are maybe a lot of me running up against the wall.
Andreas Müller:	Yep.
Justin Allen:	But aside from that, something is interesting about running up against the wall over…
Andreas Müller:	…and over…
Justin Allen:	…again, and the topic of "no me." And so I thought it would be nice to say, okay, we started in 2019 or 2020. And now it's 2024, and we're having our third (series of) talk(s). And the way that we structured the first book and then the natural following of the second book and now the third book, and it's nice that things end in threes.
Andreas Müller:	Yeah. (both laugh)
Justin Allen:	I was thinking of a nice sentence, and a nice sentence would be somebody coming to you wanting enlightenment and instead being presented with the death of the "me" or the death of the seeking or the death of enlightenment. It would be a nice thing to say: okay, now after talking with you, I've died and I am no longer a "me." And I can join the league of people that aren't there anymore. (both laugh)

But it doesn't resonate with me to say that I'm enlightened. I would never say I'm enlightened. I would never want to say, either, that there's "no me" here and that we figured out the same thing or something like that. So I would just point out that I find this topic interesting. And I was trying to think of what's so interesting, why continue to talk about it? It doesn't feel like there's a need for me to figure things out with you or through you or anybody else.

Initially, I would listen to this message much more frequently, and now it's tapered off. And my internal thought's like, "Hmm. Oh, I want to ask Andreas Müller this," that doesn't come up very often.

This third talk, sitting here, whatever talks we've had is... I have a brain that works. (both laugh) And it can come up with things to talk about. And I think it's interesting really because it's so radical from the way that we are. It's so radical from the "me" take-over and the "me-centric" way of going about life.

Enlightenment, for a while, was my main search, or at least it was there among the other big searches that I might have had. So, the confrontation with a "no me" is completely radical to anything. If I came to you saying, "Hey man, how do I find the greatest love of my life?" you'd go, "Uh, I don't know. That's not what I do, but I can talk about what I do. And what I talk about is that there's actually nobody there seeking," blah, blah, blah. So maybe you could talk about this forever in a way because it's so radically different from the 99 percent of energy that's out there that's really this kind of "me" energy. And so what you talk about is a "no me" energy or, now, I'm inventing another thing. So we could just continually talk about "no me."

Andreas Müller: Yes. You're absolutely right.

Justin Allen:

I was thinking that it's very fresh, even though it's a repetition. We talked about this in the first book, but it's not a repetition in the sense that it's just so... even because of the circumstances of "no me," of there not being anybody there with no agenda, no goal and even no history, it's a fresh new thing every time you talk about it or every way that you would talk about it.

Andreas Müller:

Yeah, absolutely.

Justin Allen:

In this conversation that we're having now, I just wanted to point out that I don't have such an ability to generate questions that I think other people might have. Sometimes, I talk about things, and I think that's repetitive or that might be what we've already covered. But this topic, just talking about "no me," and what you mean by that, or what it could be, in comparison also with "the me" energy, is almost a never-ending, interesting topic.

Andreas Müller:

Yes. Two things come to my mind. On the one hand, you are completely right. This can go on forever, and one could say as long as there's the seeking energy in one way or the other and an interest in this, this conversation can go on. And it's timeless; it'll just go on. And it'll never really change. The energetic dynamic will, in one way or the other, be like this. And it will never land or arrive. There'll never be a point when it's through.

On the other hand, there is no need for those conversations. I think that's what also happens to some people, that they almost cling to having to talk about it, to somehow keep this issue in their life. Because there don't need to be these conversations. They could also just stop. It also could have stopped after the first book. It also could have stopped after the second book or right in the middle of the first book. So it's not a need to go on or to do that, and it doesn't have a value in itself to go on like that. So it's both. It can go forever, but it could also stop instantly because none of that needs to be said to bring about something.

Justin Allen: I was pointing out more how you've been doing this for 10 years, and Tony Parsons does it for 40 years, let's say. But every time, there's a certain animation that I see. You get excited or animated sometimes in the conversation. How could that be, for you, repeating this over and over again? The audience, also, they can get excited.

Andreas Müller: Mm hmm.

Justin Allen: The excitement generally comes when they're like, "Oh my god! That's what you mean; it was never there, there was never this me thing." That's a fresh thing that you could dissect and talk about all the time.

Andreas Müller: Absolutely.

Justin Allen: I was thinking, why would it be exciting all the time after 10 years, even? It's such a fresh thing, was one answer. But also, I thought a second answer is because there's this 99 percent energetic aspect that everybody has of being "a me." And because it's so radically different and contrary, that just that, alone, generates excitement.

Andreas Müller: Yeah. Apparently, there's so much energy in this. In a way, one could say there's so much energy in this, also, because the person, which is kind of what you said, puts so much energy into itself and its life and into seeking, and this whole existential question that the person lives in. This energetic presence that's constantly, like we talked in the first talk today, there's always this tension and this inner struggle, and this is so energetic. And, of course, what this does, apparently, is to release this energy, to set it free, on this very normal ordinary way of being that would be translated into excitement, energy, and freshness.

Justin Allen: To me, even saying the sentence or the word, "no me," and grappling with that, even as a concept, just talking about that already is very intriguing. When you do a talk, you start in a way, introducing: this is it. "This is all it is. Sitting here with you in your apartment," I have a glimpse into your day-to-day life. I have a sense of what it's like to be living in your situation. And you come across, and the whole atmosphere here comes across as being authentic; everything being authentic without any kind of hidden agenda. And I was thinking, what would be another way of saying that? And that would be: that's it. If you're bare naked, you have no agenda in your head, no ulterior motives, and you present yourself to somebody, and you'd say, "Look, this is it…"

Andreas Müller: Yeah, exactly.

Justin Allen: And I was thinking that anybody that you meet, that you can go into their house and they say "Look…" It can feel like, "Okay, this is it," but generally, you always feel like that person has something hidden or that there's something in the closet, or they have something private or something that they don't want to share. Not that you also don't want me to wander around and look through every nook and cranny of your house, but it's presented like I could or like you don't care or… not that you're actively trying to present that, but that's what I mean.

Andreas Müller: That's just the energy of it. And that's just how it is. It just is like that.

Justin Allen: Yeah, that's an interesting way to think about that common sentence from the group of people that are communicating this common sentence. It's like, "It's just this," or, "This is it, that's all that there is, it's whole and complete," blah, blah, blah.

Our first talks were always through video conference. And then we met once in Hamburg, and I went to one of your talks. And then, we had our second series of talks (also via video). And then I met you in Berlin once, briefly. And now I'm here; this is the first time that we're doing (a) face-to-face. And my perspective of it is that it is a perspective or a feeling like, "Look, it's just this. This is it."

Andreas Müller: Yep. (both laugh) Oh, beautiful! No, that's exactly how it is. Absolutely. Yeah.

Justin Allen: And even talking, too, it's kind of like, I'm not getting more, I'm not learning something new. I'm not extracting some bit that's gonna trigger something new. There's nothing other than what's available right now. If it was on Zoom and I wasn't here face to face, just that distance can create...

Andreas Müller: ...space for a lot of ideas or projections, yeah. It's funny. I just thought about what you meant when you said when you go somewhere else, there might be something hidden or something. And I thought about that. Maybe it's really this sense of dissatisfaction that no one wants to be seen with. Every "me" is constantly showing it and telling what they like, what they are suffering from, what's the problem, what to do, and how... but on the other hand, no one wants to be seen that naked, so to speak. Because when the "me" would be naked, you could actually see this sense of unfulfillment and the shame about it. And maybe that's what's basically hidden, or what is in this weird inner conflict of, "I have to bring it out. I live in that dissatisfaction, but on the other hand, I don't want anyone to see it."

Justin Allen:	Yeah, you have to present some illusion or something that at least is contrary to that dissatisfaction.
Andreas Müller:	Exactly. A story about oneself, a method, or the story of "I've achieved," or whatever. And that's not there anymore, so to speak, so there's absolutely nothing to hide. There's nothing that conflicts with itself, basically. And that would be the freedom of it.
Justin Allen:	The two examples that I have of being more intimately close to a spiritual teacher: they're on a podium, they're sitting with some spiritual type posture, and they might be clothed in some unusual way. And then they have assistants or an entourage, and then there might be a big audience. The whole thing's set up so that you don't feel like you're having an equal conversation.
Andreas Müller:	Absolutely. And I think that this hierarchy, so to speak, is set up energetically. And those things, how it apparently manifests, are just a reflection of that. It's just coming out of that and confirms that energetic dynamic.
Justin Allen:	It's also that it doesn't feel like, "This is it," in those settings. It doesn't feel like, "That's all there is." It feels like there's...
Andreas Müller:	There's more.
Justin Allen:	Yeah, there's this great thing that you need. If you ask the right question, maybe you'll get it.
Andreas Müller:	That's also the personal energy, and that's what it's about there. It's about something else. About something greater, and about something else which isn't here now. It's only theoretically here now, if you would get it; if you could be without thoughts. Oh, that's the whole aura of it. And that's again the attractive thing about it.

Justin Allen:	And even this sentence, "Be in the present moment" or "Be in the now," it's already not confirming this. It's already removed from this.
Andreas Müller:	Absolutely.
Justin Allen:	That's why I think that saying, "It's just this. It's just this," is... I get it differently, I suppose. That sentence, I guess I was never intrigued by it that much. Being here, then I thought, "Okay, yeah," that's an intriguing sentence under that context; that it's just laying it out, saying there really isn't anything hidden. That's what I think is meant also by, "I'm not teaching. I'm not here, first of all. You're also not there, so I have nothing that I can offer, and there's nothing that you could get."
Andreas Müller:	Exactly.
Justin Allen:	And that's also another way of saying, "It's just this." There's not some hidden message. There's not some hidden goal. There's not something to strive for. So it's just, I don't know, blank paper. (both laugh)
Andreas Müller:	Yeah, exactly.
Justin Allen:	You could hold a piece of paper and say, "This is all I offer is a blank piece of paper."
Andreas Müller:	Exactly. Nothing.
Justin Allen:	Yeah, that would be very unsatisfactory to somebody who wanted something. But then somebody open, I think it would be intriguing for them.
Andreas Müller:	Exactly.
Justin Allen:	Because it's so fundamentally radical from everything else out there that's always offering something other than what's there.

Andreas Müller: But as I said, there are two possible reactions to it, very simplified. One is disappointment and go on seeking and go away from this. And for some people, apparently, there just seems to be this intriguing, adventurous resonance to the freedom about that. That's what seems to be happening. It can't be done either way, and neither way is right or wrong. But most people at this point just, "What?", turn around and give themselves an answer. "It's a concept." Most people would say it's a concept or it's (a) mindfuck.

Justin Allen: In general, you talking about this, it just stays fresh and fun and...

Andreas Müller: Yeah. Also, here, one could almost say that it's rather a response. So, my excitement or my energy about it is actually also a response to the excitement and the energy that comes from the one who asked the question. Because, of course, if someone treats this like a concept that we can theoretically discuss, I also don't get very excited. I probably would rather not do it at all. So, this is also a dynamic that needs both sides.

Justin Allen: Yeah. I think it would be frustrating if you were talking to somebody that wouldn't be open to... that you'd have to overcome so much from that person to get them to even just entertain what you're talking about.

Andreas Müller: Oh, it wouldn't be possible. It's not fun at all. It's the person that comes with an openness. And this amount of openness, it's a story. But that's what I respond to.

Justin Allen: It's a little bit more exciting when you have somebody that was on a path of enlightenment or some kind of a path, but they were still open to hear you. And then they hear you, and then you see their energy shift a little where they're like, "Oh, fuck." Then, they get engaged in what you've said in a real sense where they're like, "Ah, okay, so you're saying something different from what I've been…"

Andreas Müller: Exactly, yeah. It's a bit like, what liberation, in the end, also is. But it's a bit like seeing the world as a baby for the first time again. That's the freshness of it.

Justin Allen: It's like when you're a child, and you find something awesome, and then you try to get your friends to come to see it, and some of them just were like, "No, fuck you. I'm not gonna go." And then you get one of them to come over, and then they see it, and then you see them enjoy what you just saw.

Andreas Müller: I thought about the excitement of even a younger child, but yeah, I get the picture. Some people ask me, do you enjoy talking about non-duality or something, and sometimes I have to say no. Because it's not that I talk about non-duality. It's not that I wake up in the morning and look forward to, "Oh, the Zoom starts in six hours. That's when I can talk about non-duality," or as I'm seeking people to whom I can talk about non-duality. So, in that sense, I don't like to talk about the concept of non-duality at all. It's only this dynamic that makes it attractive or which makes it apparently exciting or energetic. Otherwise, I'm not really interested in the idea if there's "a me" or not. And of course, sometimes it's a bit interesting what the scientists say, but that's not half as exciting as if it boils down to this very direct and energetic dynamic.

Justin Allen: If you read the newspaper and there is a scientific discovery, which aligns with this message, there's always a little bit… of, "See?"

Andreas Müller: Yeah, there's something joyful about it. (both laugh)

No, it's not that much that "See?" energy in terms of, "Ah, see, they prove it." But, there's a joy or excitement about that as well.

Justin Allen: And same in the talks, especially if it's a bigger audience, and you hear the reactions of the audience where it seems like they've caught on, or there's a flip

Andreas Müller: Usually, it's a flip to nothing.

Justin Allen: The reaction is that sometimes there's an explosion of laughter, but it seems like it's laughter where somebody had the thought or realization that you're really talking about, "That thing that I think is there isn't there. But he's not joking."

Andreas Müller: "He's not joking," also might mean, "He's not playing another game."

Justin Allen: It's not an agenda. It's not a game. It's not a persuasion.

Andreas Müller: In that sense, one could say what's presented here is much more real than any of those personal games. In some way, the person, of course, takes it deadly seriously. On the other hand, it's seen as another game to play in the playground of the personal world, and always a bit compromising and contradictory, also energetically, while this pointing to totality isn't contradictory at all, and it's not holding back. And in that sense, I mean it.

Justin Allen: Yeah.   If you had an audience of 50 people and then there's a rumbling sometimes in the audience where it seems like 15 people caught on to it together, that's also excitement, no?

Andreas Müller: That's what I meant. What usually happens, or what can happen is that your energy really goes to nothing.

Justin Allen:	What's the description of nothing that it goes silent?
Andreas Müller:	Yeah, something like silent, but also energetically silent; not only that no one says a word or something, but at some point often there's... it's in the story now.
Justin Allen:	Like where 10 people all met the wall simultaneously and energetically. I think that's also accompanied by laughter, then. Or at least it seems like somebody kind of bursts out with laughter because they...
Andreas Müller:	At some point, yeah.
Justin Allen:	Maybe it doesn't happen as often now, but in the beginning, if you would go have a talk with two people and you were supposed to be there for an hour or two hours, I can imagine that there's nothing to talk about for a lot of that time.
Andreas Müller:	To be honest, in the beginning, this hardly happened because it just happened as our conversations. It was very often rather alive.
Justin Allen:	Yeah, but that example that you gave when you went to...
Andreas Müller:	...the conference. Oh, they asked a lot of questions. My talk just was scheduled for 20 minutes, but we did more than half an hour. We were actually kicked out of the room because the next event was supposed to start, and we didn't stop. I was just very hidden and in a small place. But there were, I think, 12, 13 people there, and it was very alive. They liked it.
Justin Allen:	But if there's only two people, doesn't that slow down the... I went to Tony Parsons in Munich. It felt like an hour long of nobody saying anything.

Andreas Müller:	It depends a bit. It depends on who's coming. But when I started it, and there were only one or two people, it was actually quite alive. Maybe this would be different now because most people who would come already saw hours of my videos, but that wasn't the case in the first years.
Justin Allen:	That must be exciting, too, in a way. It's like you're communicating with interested people, but it's radical to them.
Andreas Müller:	Exactly, and that's how it was in the first years, actually; it still is, kind of. But as I said, now, often people have seen a lot of videos already. But on the other hand, as we talked about, it's always fresh and new. So, also, many people just come up with the idea, "Okay, I know it already because I've seen a lot of videos," and then they meet this freshly, and it's very different from what they thought when they just heard it. And sometimes there are silences and sometimes not at all, but it seems rather random than, "Oh, there are just five people. It'll be silent for the whole afternoon." Often enough, it isn't.
Justin Allen:	Let's say that you go for a 30-minute walk outside or something like that. And then, for you, it just occurs to you about how you spent 30 years of your life thinking that you were "a me"?
Andreas Müller:	No.
Justin Allen:	No?
Andreas Müller:	No, never.
Justin Allen:	But in the end, it never occurs to you where it's just so absurd, the...
Andreas Müller:	No, not at all. Because I don't think it's absurd. The surprise is that that was it, too. I really can't

energetically look back and make this distinction between before and after for myself. It was all whole and complete.

Justin Allen: Not even that. Just that there is that "me" energy out there; that there are so many people that think that they're...

Andreas Müller: No. I really don't go there.

Justin Allen: I guess if I were to think of myself as not being here, but everybody else is thinking that they're there, it just would feel like that's it; like that's also it.

Andreas Müller: Oh no, of course not. Because for the person, this is fundamentally different.

Justin Allen: I meant trying to make it seem like if you're convinced that you're there, that somehow that's significant, or weird, or that that shouldn't happen, or that it's absurd that it's happening; that there are so many people that are with "me" energy going around. It doesn't seem different. Or, if there were no "me's," nothing would change anyway.

Andreas Müller: Yeah. As I said, I don't think it's absurd. Because I also thought it wasn't absurd that I was seeking, because of what seemed to have happened, that I felt like "a me," whatever that is.

Justin Allen: With the way that you're describing it, it's not comparable to, "Oh, I was so stupid when I was younger."

Andreas Müller: No, not at all. Being a me was also it. There never was anyone, and it was also it. I wasn't stupid back then. It wasn't dumb that I was experiencing myself as "a me" and seeking. It was what seemed to have happened. It was whole and complete, and it wasn't anyone's mistake, and there was "no one" who could have known better or seen through the illusion or anything. Not at all. It just was what seemed to have happened until it wasn't the case anymore, so to speak. And this didn't bring about the change that I was hoping for when I was a seeker. What the seeker wants will never happen. It can't.

Justin Allen:

Yeah. That's the radical confrontation is that, generally, people are confronting this from a seeking position, still thinking that this is going to help them on their journey.

Andreas Müller:

To arrive at what they think will lead to a personal experience.

Justin Allen:

In some way, this is going to help. But if you meet this confrontation enough times or under whatever circumstance is necessary, then you're confronted with, "Oh, no, this isn't another..."

Andreas Müller:

Exactly.

Justin Allen:

"Nobody's lending me a helping hand here."

Andreas Müller:

Exactly. It's not another path to rip off the illusion. It's not a harsh way to rip off the illusion, in contrast to a soft path. It's completely out of that.

Justin Allen:

Yeah. And then it's paradoxical in a sense because you could say, "Oh man, I feel so alone because there's really nobody helping me now." I would say I felt more alone thinking that I had to depend on somebody to help me get enlightened.

Andreas Müller:

Yeah, I've heard both.

Justin Allen:

It feels very weird to think that you have to meet a guru or that you have to do all these steps to become enlightened.

Andreas Müller:	It didn't feel weird to me back then. To me, this idea was very comforting; that there is someone out there who can guide me and carry me in a very romantic idea whenever I'm down, so to speak. That was my idea. So, for me, the idea of there being someone who can help me was rather comforting
Justin Allen:	The difference between Americans and Germans. (both laugh)
Andreas Müller:	Still looking for the strong figure outside. (both laugh) Everyone has their approach. And I know some people who would say after meeting this message, they felt deadly alone because of what you just said. They noticed that there was nothing out there that could help me (them) because, in a way, they lost already trust in everything else. So, a lot of people believe to have is this message because everything else is already gone. And then this message says, "Well, I can't help you." This could also be translated into total aloneness. Even in that, there's a freedom.
Justin Allen:	The reason why it doesn't feel lonely also is because if there's somebody enlightened, it's the same as feeling like, "I wish I had money as that guy does." It's like that concept of FOMO, fear of missing out. And this levels everything. So, in that sense, it feels like, because it levels everything out, that you can't be alone anymore.
Andreas Müller:	Yeah, I mean, that's what this message is saying in the end. Of course, it levels all out. And there isn't anyone or anything separate from it and lost from it.
Justin Allen:	It doesn't seem lonely, whereas all those other teachings or messages always gave me a sense of loneliness because there's a small percentage that has achieved it. And it feels like there's something to achieve. And if you don't achieve it, then you're

left out of the wall of...

Andreas Müller: ...paradise. Yeah, absolutely.

Justin Allen: This is the communism approach. (both laugh)

Andreas Müller: It's all or nothing. Communists, anarchic, individual: it levels those all out.

Justin Allen: If we turn this into a book to share, also, the first one was called No-Point Perspective and the second one was No-Point. (both laugh) And the third one, I want to call it No, but you're not convinced.

Andreas Müller: Not 100 percent. Of course, it would make sense. But this message isn't... it's not really "no."

Justin Allen: Yeah, your hesitation is because you don't want to be confined to one side of a dichotomy.

Andreas Müller: My idea was No-Yes or something. Because, as I said, that's not the message. The message isn't "no." That would be nihilism.

Justin Allen: But, "No-Point," wasn't the message, either. (laughs)

Andreas Müller: But it made sense that we had this first book, "No-Point Perspective," and then the second book, there wasn't a point anymore to talk about. But just, "No," it's a... (both laugh)

Justin Allen: What if it's, "No-," with the hyphen, still?

Andreas Müller: Maybe the No makes much more sense from your approach to it.

Justin Allen: There are two ways that it makes sense. So, one way is that it just turned out that the first book was "No-Point Perspective." I pulled that title out from… it was in the context of me grappling with your message. Then, in the next one, there's less to say, the book is half the size. So it seemed like, what if we just take away a word from it?

Andreas Müller: But the energy of it was also quite… the pointlessness was more obvious.

Justin Allen: And then, the third one… We're having three and a half conversations or four conversations. (laughs) And so it's going to be even less than the other one. So then, in that sense, the title should be less. And in that way, it's fair also to say it's "No-Yes," because it's still fewer letters.

Andreas Müller: It's still shorter, yeah. I'm fine now that we talked about it, and this conversation might remain in the book. I'm fine with it, that this message is not, "no." It's a simultaneous yes and no.

Justin Allen: But also the message isn't really, "no-point perspective," because that still implies a perspective.

Andreas Müller: No, I don't think so, that "no-point perspective" implies a perspective because it's a no-point perspective. (laughs)

Justin Allen: You think it is the message?

Andreas Müller: No, because there is no message. But of course, when I say, "there is no one," this also means that there is no perspective. That's the funny thing with this. On the one hand, there is "no one." On the other hand, it's very direct and natural. That's the problem. So, how to say, then, that it's direct and alive, apparently, but at the same time nothing and not a perspective? That's what I liked about No-Point Perspective. Of course, it's not a perspective, but we talk about something very direct and not conceptual.

Justin Allen:	Yeah.
Andreas Müller:	It's really, "there is no one."
Justin Allen:	In that sense, no title is good. It's just some are maybe better than others. No-Point Perspective is better than My-Point Perspective. (both laugh)
Andreas Müller:	But this message is yes and no. Real and unreal.
Justin Allen:	When you say things like real and unreal, that's always just the same as nothing and everything.
Andreas Müller:	Exactly. Yes and no.
Justin Allen:	I always found yes and no, or nothing and everything, or real and unreal... for me, that doesn't spark anything.
Andreas Müller:	Of course, because, for the person, these are just words which so obviously don't say anything, really. And it sounds so general. It's so much not saying something. This is nothing and everything. "All right. Well, how can I become happy? Should I have pizza or rice?" It's real and unreal. "Yeah, all right, I've heard that, but rice or pizza?"
Justin Allen:	If we ended up doing a fourth one, then we'd have to come up with a whole new title.
Andreas Müller:	Well, maybe in the fourth one we could add the "yes" to it. (laughs)
Justin Allen:	If the fourth one was No-Yes, then what would the fifth one be?
Andreas Müller:	Oh, I have no idea. (both laugh)
	Nothing and everything. Everything and nothing.

Justin Allen: When you have your talks, you usually end with where you say, "That's it. This is it..."

Andreas Müller: Yeah. (both laugh) I usually say, "So, well, I guess that's it."

Justin Allen: That's a good ending.

Andreas Müller: Usually I give a small speech, also.

Justin Allen: Yeah, you usually say, "That's it. This is it."

Andreas Müller: "There's nothing to get. There is no message. It's all whole and complete. There's nothing to take home. There's no suggestion," and all those things that I'm saying. Yeah. And then usually I say, "Thanks a lot." Thank you very much.

Justin Allen: Yeah, thanks.

Andreas Müller was born and grew up in Southern Germany. After having become a spiritual seeker in his teens, he met Tony Parsons in 2009. Since 2011, Andreas has been holding talks and intensives throughout the world.

Justin Allen is an architect in Berlin, Germany. Justin has a background in philosophy and he is originally from upstate New York.